PRISONERS OF TIME

April 1994

Report of the National Education Commission on Time and Learning

For sale by the U.S. Government Printing Office
Superintendent of Documents, Mail Stop: SSOP, Washington, DC 20402-9328

LETTER OF TRANSMITTAL

April 1994

The Honorable Albert Gore
President
United States Senate

The Honorable Thomas S. Foley
Speaker
United States House of Representatives

The Honorable Richard W. Riley
Secretary
United States Department of Education

Gentlemen:

Public Law 102-62 (The Education Council Act of 1991) established the National Education Commission on Time and Learning as an independent advisory body and called for a comprehensive review of the relationship between time and learning in the nation's schools. The legislation created a nine-member Commission (three each to be appointed by the Secretary of Education, the President of the Senate, and the Speaker of the House of Representatives) and directed the Commission to prepare a report on its findings by April 1994. We are pleased to present that report for your consideration.

In the 24 months since the Commission was established, we have met 18 times to discuss the issues outlined in our statute. We visited 19 schools and education programs across the United States. We listened to more than 150 teachers, administrators, parents, students and other experts on education. We worked with school officials in Japan and Germany to complete two fact-finding visits to schools and research institutes in those countries.

Our conclusions and recommendations speak for themselves. Time is the missing element in our great national debate about learning and the need for higher standards for all students. Our schools and the people involved with them—students, teachers, administrators, parents, and staff—are prisoners of time, captives of the school clock and calendar. We have been asking the impossible of our students— that they learn as much as their foreign peers while spending only half as much time in core academic subjects. The reform movement of the last decade is destined to founder unless it is harnessed to more time for learning.

We want to thank each of you for your confidence that we could complete this challenging assignment. Your support helped us complete the task on schedule. We tried to be straightforward in our discussions with each other and in our recommendations about what needs to be done. Although each of us may harbor minor reservations about details of this report, we are unanimous in supporting its broad themes and recommendations.

Finally, we want to acknowledge the work of our staff under the able leadership of its executive director, Milton Goldberg. Amidst the pressure of deadlines and *honest differences of opinion about how to proceed on these complex issues, the staff*

unfailingly came through as the professionals they are.

John Hodge Jones
Commission Chairman
Superintendent
Murfreesboro City Schools
Murfreesboro, Tennessee

Carol Schwartz
Commission Vice Chairman
Former Member
D.C. City Council and Board of Education
Washington, D. C.

Hon. Michael J. Barrett
State Senator
Commonwealth of Massachusetts
Cambridge, Massachusetts

Norman E. Higgins
Principal
Piscataquis Community High School
Guilford, Maine

B. Marie Byers
President
Washington County Board of Education
Hagerstown, Maryland

William E. Shelton
President
Eastern Michigan University
Ypsilanti, Michigan

Christopher T. Cross
Director, Education Initiative
The Business Roundtable
Washington, D.C.

Glenn R. Walker
Principal
Clifton-Clyde High School & Clyde Elementary
Clyde, Kansas

Denis P. Doyle
Senior Fellow
The Hudson Institute
Chevy Chase, Maryland

PRISONERS OF TIME

IF EXPERIENCE,
RESEARCH, AND COM-
MON SENSE TEACH
NOTHING ELSE, THEY
CONFIRM THE TRUISM
THAT PEOPLE LEARN
AT DIFFERENT RATES,
AND IN DIFFERENT
WAYS WITH DIFFERENT
SUBJECTS.

Learning in America is a prisoner of time. For the past 150 years, American public schools have held time constant and let learning vary. The rule, only rarely voiced, is simple: learn what you can in the time we make available. It should surprise no one that some bright, hard-working students do reasonably well. Everyone else—from the typical student to the dropout—runs into trouble.

Time is learning's warden. Our time-bound mentality has fooled us all into believing that schools can educate all of the people all of the time in a school year of 180 six-hour days. The consequence of our self-deception has been to ask the impossible of our students. We expect them to learn as much as their counterparts abroad in only half the time.

As Oliver Hazard Perry said in a famous dispatch from the War of 1812: "We have met the enemy and they are [h]ours."

If experience, research, and common sense teach nothing else, they confirm the truism that people learn at different rates, and in different ways with different subjects. But we have put the cart before the horse: our schools and the people involved with them—students, parents, teachers, administrators, and staff—are captives of clock and calendar. The boundaries of student growth are defined by schedules for bells, buses, and vacations instead of standards for students and learning.

CONTROL BY THE CLOCK

The degree to which today's American school is controlled by the dynamics of clock and calendar is surprising, even to people who understand school operations:

- With few exceptions, schools open and close their doors at fixed times in the morning and early afternoon—a school in one district might open at 7:30 a.m. and close at 2:15 p.m.; in another, the school day might run from 8:00 in the morning until 3:00 in the afternoon.

- With few exceptions, the school year lasts nine months, beginning in late summer and ending in late spring.

- According to the National Center for Education Statistics, schools typically offer a six-period day, with about 5.6 hours of classroom time a day.

- No matter how complex or simple the school subject—literature, shop, physics, gym, or algebra—the schedule assigns each an impartial national average of 51 minutes per class period, no matter how well or poorly students comprehend the material.

- The norm for required school attendance, according to the Council of Chief State School Officers, is 180 days. Eleven states permit school terms of 175 days or less; only one state requires more than 180.

- Secondary school graduation requirements are universally based on seat time—"Carnegie units," a standard of measurement representing one credit for completion of a one-year course meeting daily.

- Staff salary increases are typically tied to time—to seniority and the number of hours of graduate work completed.

- Despite the obsession with time, little attention is paid to how it is used: in 42 states examined by the Commission, only 41 percent of secondary school time must be spent on core academic subjects.

The results are predictable. The school clock governs how families organize their lives, how administrators oversee their schools, and how teachers work their way through the curriculum. Above all, it governs how material is presented to students and the opportunity they have to comprehend and master it.

This state of affairs explains a universal phenomenon during the last quarter of the academic year: as time runs out on them, frustrated teachers face the task of cramming large portions of required material into a fraction of the time intended for it. As time runs out on the teacher, perceptive students are left to wonder about the integrity of an instructional system that behaves, year-in and year-out, as though the last chapters of their textbooks are not important.

A FOUNDATION OF SAND

Unyielding and relentless, the time available in a uniform six-hour day and a 180-day year is the unacknowledged design flaw in American education. By relying on time as the metric for school organization and curriculum, we have built a learning enterprise on a foundation of sand, on five premises educators know to be false.

The first is the assumption that students arrive at school ready to learn in the same way, on the same schedule, all in rhythm with each other.

The second is the notion that academic time can be used for nonacademic purposes with no effect on learning.

Next is the pretense that because yesterday's calendar was good enough for us, it should be good enough for our children—despite major changes in the larger society.

Fourth is the myth that schools can be transformed without giving teachers the time they need to retool themselves and reorganize their work.

Finally, we find a new fiction: it is reasonable to expect "world-class academic performance" from our students within the time-bound system that is already failing them.

These five assumptions are a recipe for a kind of slow-motion social suicide.

THE REALITIES OF THE GLOBAL ECONOMY

In our agrarian and industrial past, when most Americans worked on farms or in factories, society could live with the consequences of time-bound education. Able students usually could do well and accomplish a lot. Most others did enough to get by and enjoyed some modest academic success. Dropouts learned little but could still look forward to productive unskilled and even semi-skilled work. Society can no longer live with these results.

The reality of today's world is that the global economy provides few decent jobs for the poorly educated. Today, a new standard for an educated citizenry is required, a standard suited to the 21st century, not the 19th or the 20th. Americans must be as knowledgeable, competent, and inventive as any people in the world. All of our citizens, not just a few, must be able to think for a living. Indeed, our students should do more than meet the standard; they should set it. The stakes are very high. Our people not only have to survive amidst today's changes, they have to be able to create tomorrow's.

The approach of a new century offers the opportunity to create an education system geared to the demands of a new age and a different world. In the school of the future, learning—in the form of high, measurable standards of student performance—must become the fixed goal. Time must become an adjustable resource.

LIMITED TIME FRUSTRATES ASPIRATIONS FOR REFORM

For the past decade, Americans have mounted a major effort to reform education, an effort that continues today, its energy undiminished. The reform movement has captured the serious attention of the White House, Congress, state capitals and local school boards. It has enjoyed vigorous support from teachers and administrators. It has been applauded by parents, the public, and the business community. It is one of the major issues on the nation's domestic agenda and one of the American people's most pressing concerns.

Today, this reform movement is in the midst of impressive efforts to reach National Education Goals by defining higher standards for content and student achievement and framing new systems of accountability to ensure that schools educate and students learn. These activities are aimed at comprehensive education reform—improving every dimension of schooling so that students leave school equipped to earn a decent living, enjoy the richness of life, and participate responsibly in local and national affairs.

As encouraging as these ambitious goals are, this Commission is convinced that we cannot get there from here with the amount of time now available and the way we now use it. Limited time will frustrate our aspirations. Misuse of time will undermine our best efforts.

Opinion polls indicate that most Americans, and the vast majority of teachers, support higher academic standards. Some, however, fear that rigorous standards might further disadvantage our most vulnerable children. In our current time-bound system, this fear is well founded. Applied inflexibly, high standards could cause great mischief.

But today's practices—different standards for different students and promotion by age and grade according to the calendar—are a hoax, cruel deceptions of both students and society. Time, the missing element in the school reform debate, is also the overlooked solution to the standards problem. Holding all students to the same high standards means that some students will need more time, just as some may require less. Standards are then not a barrier to success but a mark of accomplishment. Used wisely and well, time can be the academic equalizer.

TIME: NOT A NEW ISSUE

The federal government, concerned about student achievement in the United States, directed this Commission to conduct a comprehensive examination of the broad relationship between time and learning. Time is not a new issue in the education debate, but an age-old concern. As our work progressed, we realized that a report published precisely a century ago is painfully relevant to our inquiry.

In 1894, U. S. Commissioner of Education William T. Harris argued in his annual report that it was a great mistake to abandon the custom of keeping urban schools open nearly the entire year. He complained of a "distinct loss this year, the average number of days of school having been reduced from 193.5 to 191," and wrote:

> [T]he constant tendency [has been] toward a reduction of time. First, the Saturday morning session was discontinued; then the summer vacations were lengthened; the morning sessions were shortened; the afternoon sessions were curtailed; new holidays were introduced; provisions were made for a single session on stormy days, and for closing the schools to allow teachers...to attend teachers' institutes...

> The boy of today must attend school 11.1 years in order to receive as much instruction, quantitatively, as the boy of fifty years ago received in 8 years... It is scarcely necessary to look further than this for the explanation for the greater amount of work accomplished...in the German and French than in the American schools...

Published 100 years ago, that document could have been issued last week.

THE IMPERATIVE FOR AN AMERICAN TRANSFORMATION

What lies before the American people—nothing short of reinventing the American school—will require unprecedented effort. This report concludes with several recommendations about time. The simple truth, however, is that none of them will make much difference unless there is a transformation in attitudes about education.

The transformation we seek requires a widespread conviction in our society that *learning matters*. Learning matters, not simply because it leads to better jobs or produces national wealth, but because it enriches the human spirit and advances social health.

The human ability to learn and grow is the cornerstone of a civil and humane society. Until our nation embraces the importance of education as an investment in our common future—the foundation of domestic tranquility and the cure for our growing anxiety about the civility of this society—nothing will really change.

Certainly nothing will change as long as education remains a convenient whipping boy camouflaging larger failures of national will and shortcomings in public and private leadership.

As a people, we are obsessed with international economic comparisons. We fail to acknowledge that a nation's economic power often depends on the strength of its education system. Parents, grandparents, employers—even children—understand and believe in the power of learning. The strongest message this Commission can send to the American people is that education must become a new national obsession, as powerful as sports and entertainment, if we are to avoid a spiral of economic and social decline.

But if this transformation requires unprecedented national effort, it does not require unprecedented thinking about school operations. Common sense suffices: American students must have more time for learning. The six-hour, 180-day school year should be relegated to museums, an exhibit from our education past. Both learners and teachers need more time—not to do more of the same, but to use all time in new, different, and better ways. The key to liberating learning lies in unlocking time.

AN URBAN ELEMENTARY SCHOOL FOR THE NEXT CENTURY

NEW STANLEY ELEMENTARY SCHOOL IN KANSAS CITY, KANSAS IS TYPICAL OF MANY URBAN ELEMENTARY SCHOOLS—TWO-THIRDS OF ITS 360 STUDENTS ARE FROM MINORITY BACKGROUNDS (AFRICAN-AMERICAN, NATIVE AMERICAN, AND HISPANIC) AND 75 PERCENT OF ITS ENROLLMENT IS POOR ENOUGH TO QUALIFY FOR FREE OR REDUCED-PRICE LUNCHES.

WITH THE HELP OF A GRANT FROM THE RJR NABISCO FOUNDATION'S "NEXT CENTURY SCHOOLS" PROGRAM, THE SCHOOL DEVELOPED AN INNOVATIVE BLUEPRINT FOR LEARNING THAT EXTENDS THE SCHOOL YEAR, PROVIDES FOR A LONGER SCHOOL DAY, GROUPS TEACHERS WITH THE SAME STUDENTS FOR SEVERAL YEARS, AND ENCOURAGES TEACHER COLLABORATION.

AT THE HEART OF THE EFFORT: HIGH EXPECTATIONS FOR ALL STUDENTS, BACKED UP BY INNOVATIVE APPROACHES COMBINING THE BEST FEATURES OF THE EFFECTIVE SCHOOLS MOVEMENT, THEORIES OF STUDENT EFFECTIVENESS AND AUTONOMY DEVELOPED AT HARVARD UNIVERSITY, AND THE PIONEERING WORK OF YALE CHILD DEVELOPMENT EXPERT JAMES COMER.

AMONG THE FEATURES THAT HELP THE SCHOOL WORK: NEW STANLEY IS IN SESSION ALMOST 11 MONTHS A YEAR, WITH STUDENTS ATTENDING SCHOOL FOR 205 DAYS, AND TEACHERS ON DUTY FOR 226. SCHOOL SESSIONS RUN FOR TEN WEEKS, FOLLOWED BY A WEEK OF TEACHER TRAINING AND PLANNING. "YOU DON'T GET WELL-DEVELOPED PROFESSIONALS WITH TWO INSERVICE DAYS A YEAR," SAYS PRINCIPAL DONNA HARDY.

TEAMS OF TEACHERS, MOREOVER, ARE ASSIGNED TO THE SAME STUDENTS FOR THREE-YEAR PERIODS. TO MEET THE NEEDS OF WORKING PARENTS, NEW STANLEY OFFERS BEFORE- AND AFTER-SCHOOL PROGRAMS SUCH AS DAY CARE, TUTORING AND ENRICHMENT, RECREATION, AND BREAKFASTS.

DOES ANY OF THIS MAKE ANY DIFFERENCE? SO FAR THE SIGNS ARE ENCOURAGING. IN JUSTIFYING THESE CHANGES, THE SCHOOL DISTRICT GUARANTEED THAT ALL STUDENTS ENTERING MIDDLE SCHOOL FROM NEW STANLEY WOULD DO SO AT OR ABOVE GRADE LEVEL. TO DATE, THE WARRANTY HAS BEEN KEPT.

DIMENSIONS OF THE TIME CHALLENGE

THE TRADITIONAL
SCHOOL DAY, ORIGINAL-
LY INTENDED FOR CORE
ACADEMIC LEARNING,
NOW HOUSES A WHOLE
SET OF REQUIREMENTS
FOR WHAT HAS BEEN
CALLED "THE NEW WORK
OF THE SCHOOLS."

There is an urgency about the issue of time and learning that is felt by the public but not yet reflected in the responses of many education officials. On these issues, the American people may be ahead of their schools.

Opinion polls reviewed by the Commission reveal a revolution in public attitudes about time, schools, and the role of schools in the community. According to recent polls findings:

- After nearly 40 years of opposing a longer school year, 52 percent of Americans today favor students' spending more time in school.

- A plurality favors increasing the number of days in the year as opposed to the number of hours in the day (47 versus 33 percent).

- A large majority (62 percent) supports providing after-school care for the children of working parents.

- Americans have reached a national consensus on the importance of pre-school programs to help low-income and minority children get ready for school (85 percent support).

Public opinion experts also report that when Americans are asked to identify their worries about elementary and secondary education, their primary concern is the quality of education provided to their children. Harnessed then, in the public mind, are two powerful forces for reform: a belief that the paramount issue in American education is quality and a dawning consensus, just now being articulated, that school time, broadly conceived, is quality's ally.

The response of America's education leaders to the imperative for school reform is impressive. Both Presidents Bush and Clinton were early advocates of adopting ambitious National Education Goals (see sidebar, next page). These goals enjoy bipartisan support in the Congress and in state houses. The National Council on Education Standards and Testing called in 1992 for the development of new learning standards for all students and voluntary national tests to reinforce them. The content standards movement sweeping American education promises to revolutionize learning.

Based on its 24-month investigation, however, the Commission is convinced that five unresolved issues present insurmountable barriers to these efforts to improve learning. They define the dimensions of the time challenge facing American schools:

- The fixed clock and calendar is a fundamental design flaw that must be changed.

- Academic time has been stolen to make room for a host of nonacademic activities.

- Today's school schedule must be modified to respond to the great changes that have reshaped American life outside school.

- Educators do not have the time they need to do their job properly.

- Mastering world-class standards will require more time for almost all students.

THE DESIGN FLAW

Decades of school improvement efforts have foundered on a fundamental design flaw, the assumption that learning can be doled out by the clock and defined by the

NATIONAL EDUCATION GOALS

IN 1989, THE NATION'S GOVERNORS ADOPTED SIX NATIONAL EDUCATION GOALS, WHICH WERE INCORPORATED INTO "GOALS 2000": EDUCATE AMERICA ACT. THE GOALS 2000 LEGISLATION ULTIMATELY DEFINED EIGHT GOALS:

BY THE YEAR 2000:

1. SCHOOL READINESS: ALL CHILDREN IN AMERICA WILL START SCHOOL READY TO LEARN.

2. SCHOOL COMPLETION: THE HIGH SCHOOL GRADUATION RATE WILL INCREASE TO AT LEAST 90 PERCENT.

3. STUDENT ACHIEVEMENT AND CITIZENSHIP: AMERICAN STUDENTS WILL LEAVE GRADES FOUR, EIGHT, AND TWELVE HAVING DEMONSTRATED COMPETENCY IN CHALLENGING SUBJECT MATTER—INCLUDING ENGLISH, MATHEMATICS, SCIENCE, FOREIGN LANGUAGES, CIVICS AND GOVERNMENT, ECONOMICS, ARTS, HISTORY, AND GEOGRAPHY —[AND LEAVE SCHOOL] PREPARED FOR RESPONSIBLE CITIZENSHIP, FURTHER LEARNING, AND PRODUCTIVE EMPLOYMENT.

4. TEACHER EDUCATION AND PROFESSIONAL DEVELOPMENT: THE NATION'S TEACHING FORCE WILL HAVE ACCESS TO PROGRAMS FOR THE CONTINUED IMPROVEMENT OF THEIR PROFESSIONAL SKILLS AND THE OPPORTUNITY TO ACQUIRE THE KNOWLEDGE AND SKILLS NEEDED TO ... PREPARE ... STUDENTS FOR THE NEXT CENTURY.

5. MATHEMATICS AND SCIENCE: U.S. STUDENTS WILL BE FIRST IN THE WORLD IN SCIENCE AND MATHEMATICS ACHIEVEMENT.

6. ADULT LITERACY AND LIFELONG LEARNING: EVERY ADULT AMERICAN WILL BE LITERATE AND WILL POSSESS THE KNOWLEDGE AND SKILLS NECESSARY TO COMPETE IN A GLOBAL ECONOMY AND EXERCISE THE RIGHTS AND RESPONSIBILITIES OF CITIZENSHIP.

7. SAFE, DISCIPLINED, AND ALCOHOL- AND DRUG-FREE SCHOOLS: EVERY SCHOOL IN AMERICA WILL BE FREE OF DRUGS, VIOLENCE, AND THE UNAUTHORIZED PRESENCE OF FIREARMS AND ALCOHOL AND WILL OFFER A DISCIPLINED ENVIRONMENT CONDUCIVE TO LEARNING.

8. PARENTAL PARTICIPATION: EVERY SCHOOL WILL PROMOTE PARTNERSHIPS THAT WILL INCREASE PARENTAL INVOLVEMENT AND PARTICIPATION IN PROMOTING THE SOCIAL, EMOTIONAL, AND ACADEMIC GROWTH OF CHILDREN.

calendar. Research confirms common sense. Some students take three to six times longer than others to learn the same thing. Yet students are caught in a time trap—processed on an assembly line scheduled to the minute. Our usage of time virtually assures the failure of many students.

Under today's practices, high-ability students are forced to spend more time than they need on a curriculum developed for students of moderate ability. Many become bored, unmotivated, and frustrated. They become prisoners of time.

Struggling students are forced to move with the class and receive less time than they need to master the material. They are penalized with poor grades. They are pushed on to the next task before they are ready. They fall further and further behind and begin living with a powerful dynamic of school failure that is reinforced as long as they remain enrolled or until they drop out. They also become prisoners of time.

What of "average" students? They get caught in the time trap as well. Conscientious teachers discover that the effort to motivate the most capable and help those in difficulty robs them of time for the rest of the class. Typical students are prisoners of time too.

The paradox is that the more the school tries to be fair in allocating time, the more unfair the consequences. Providing equal time for students who need more time guarantees unequal results. If we genuinely intend to give every student an equal opportunity to reach high academic standards, we must understand that some students will require unequal amounts of time, i.e., they will need additional time.

One response to the difficulty of juggling limited time to meet special needs has been the development of "pull-out programs," in which students needing reinforcement or more advanced work are "pulled out" of the regular classroom for supplemental work. Attractive in theory, these programs, in practice, replace regular classroom time in the same subject. They add little additional time for learning. Students deserve an education that matches their needs every hour

of the school day, not just an hour or two a week. Pull-out programs are a poor part-time solution to a serious full-time problem.

ACADEMIC TIME AND NONACADEMIC ACTIVITIES

The traditional school day, originally intended for core academic learning, must now fit in a whole set of requirements for what has been called "the new work of the schools"—education about personal safety, consumer affairs, AIDS, conservation and energy, family life, driver's training—as well as traditional nonacademic activities, such as counseling, gym, study halls, homeroom, lunch and pep rallies. The school day, nominally six periods, is easily reduced at the secondary level to about three hours of time for core academic instruction.

Most Americans believe these activities are worthwhile. But where do schools find the time? Within a constrained school day, it can only come from robbing Peter to pay Paul.

Time lost to extracurricular activities is another universal complaint of educators. A 1990 survey of Missouri principals indicated that student activities can deny students the equivalent of seven school days a year. According to these principals, the academic calendar falls victim to demands from athletics, clubs, and other activities. Who is to say that these pastimes are not beneficial to many students? But how much academic time can be stolen from Peter to pay Paul?

OUT-OF-SCHOOL INFLUENCES

Over the last generation, American life has changed profoundly. Many of our children are in deep trouble.

Family structure has changed dramatically. Half of American children spend some portion of their childhood in a single-parent home, and family time with children has declined 40 percent since World War II.

A SCHOOL YEAR THAT NEVER REALLY ENDS

AT BEACON DAY SCHOOL (ELE-MENTARY) AND BEACON HIGH SCHOOL IN OAKLAND, CALIFORNIA, THE SCHOOL YEAR NEVER REALLY ENDS. AT THESE PRIVATE SCHOOLS, THE SCHOOL DAY IS OVER TEN HOURS LONG. THERE IS NO SET VACATION PERIOD; PARENTS PLAN VACATIONS TO FIT FAMILY NEEDS; STU-DENTS WORK IN TEAMS BY ACHIEVE-MENT LEVEL, NOT AGE; LETTER GRADES ARE UNKNOWN IN THE ELEMENTARY SCHOOL; AND STUDENTS SPEND SIX TO EIGHT HOURS A WEEK ON ART, MUSIC, DANCE, DRAMA OR MARTIAL ARTS. "THERE'S NO SUMMER VACATION, SO THERE'S EXTRA TIME TO LEARN,"10-YEAR-OLD COLIN GAGE TOLD THE COMMISSION.

LESLIE MEDINE, CO-DIRECTOR OF THE SCHOOLS, DESCRIBED DIFFERENT APPROACHES TO THE TWO LEVELS OF SCHOOLING. BASED ON STUDENTS' DEVELOPMENTAL NEEDS, SHE TESTI-FIED, DAY SCHOOL STUDENTS ATTEND SCHOOL 240 DAYS A YEAR, WHEREAS HIGH SCHOOL STUDENTS ATTEND 215. BOTH SCHOOLS ARE OPEN FROM 7:30 A.M. TO 5:00 P.M., 240 DAYS A YEAR, WITH TEACHERS WORKING ON FLEXIBLE SCHEDULES FOR 210 DAYS. EVERY SIX WEEKS, AT LEAST TWO TEACHERS ARE ON LEAVE THROUGHOUT THE YEAR, THEIR PLACES TAKEN BY EIGHT PERMA-NENT, FULL-TIME, SUBSTITUTE TEACH-ERS KNOWN AS "FLEXES."

The workforce is different. Of the 53 million women working in the United States in 1991, 20.8 million had children under the age of 17, including nearly 9 million with children under age six.

Society is more diverse and rapidly becoming more so. By the year 2010, 40 percent of all children in this country will be members of minority groups. The nation's big city schools are already coping with a new generation of immigrant children, largely non-English speaking, rivaling in size the great European immigrations of the 19th and early 20th centuries.

Income inequality is growing. One fifth of all children, and nearly half of all African-American children, are born into poverty today. The United States leads advanced nations in poverty, single-parent families, and mortality rates for those under age 25. Poverty is not simply an urban phenomenon. The number of rural children living in poverty far exceeds the number living in cities.

Technology threatens to widen the gap between the "haves" and the "have-nots." The wealthiest 25-30 percent of American families have a computer at home today, leading to a new phenomenon, preschoolers who can use computers before they can read a book.

Anxiety about crime-ridden streets is a daily reality in many communities. Suicide and homicide are the leading cause of death for young men. For some students, the streets are a menace. For many, the family that should be their haven is itself in trouble. Still others arrive at school hungry, unwashed, and frightened by the plagues of modern life—drug and alcohol abuse, teenage pregnancy, and AIDs.

According to a 1992 study completed at Stanford University, veteran teachers are well aware that today's students bring many more problems to school than children did a generation ago. Today's students receive less support outside school and increasingly exhibit destructive behavior ranging from drug and alcohol abuse to gang membership and precocious sexual activity. According to a recent Harris poll, 51 percent of teachers single out "children who are left on their own after school" as the primary explanation for students' difficulties in class. The same poll reports that 12 percent of elementary school children (30 percent in middle school and nearly 40 percent in high school) care for themselves after the school day ends.

But the school itself is a prisoner of time. Despite the dedication of their staffs, schools are organized as though none of this has happened. It is clear that schools cannot be all things to all people—teachers cannot be parents, police officers, physicians, and addiction or employment counselors. But neither can they ignore massive problems. It is time to face the obvious. In many communities, when children are not with their families, the next best place for them is the school.

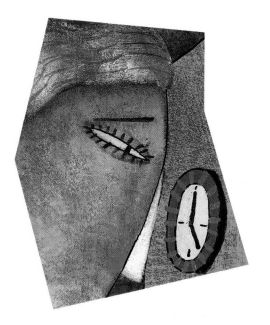

TIME AS A PROBLEM FOR EDUCATORS

The corollary to Murphy's Law holds in schools just as it does in life—everything takes longer than you expect. School reform is no exception. While restructuring time, schools need time to restructure. Perversely, according to a recent RAND study, the reallocation of time collides directly with forces of the *status quo*—entrenched school practices; rules and regulations; traditions of school decision-making; and collective bargaining. The greatest resistance of all is found in the conviction that the only valid use of teachers' time is "in front of the class;" the assumption that reading, planning, collaboration with other teachers and professional development are somehow a waste of time.

In light of this, the following findings are particularly troubling:

- According to a RAND study, new teaching strategies can require as much as 50 hours of instruction, practice and coaching before teachers become comfortable with them.

- A study of successful urban schools indicates they needed up to 50 days of external technical assistance for coaching and strengthening staff skills through professional development.

IS THERE A BETTER WAY?

MEETING STUDENT NEEDS IN THE SOUTHWEST

EMERSON ELEMENTARY SCHOOL SITS IN ALBUQUERQUE, NEW MEXICO, THE NATION'S 13TH LARGEST SCHOOL DISTRICT, LIKE A KIND OF EDUCATION UNITED NATIONS—SOME 20 LANGUAGES AND CULTURES ARE REPRESENTED IN THE SCHOOL. NINE OUT OF TEN OF ITS 800 STUDENTS QUALIFY FOR THE FREE LUNCH PROGRAM, AND THE SCHOOL HAS TO COPE WITH ANNUAL STUDENT TURNOVER AS HIGH AS 90 PERCENT.

THE YEAR-ROUND EDUCATION PROGRAM SEEMS TO BE WORKING WELL IN EMERSON, WHICH OPERATES A 12-WEEK-ON, 15-DAY-OFF, MULTI-TRACK SCHEDULE WITH THE ENTIRE SCHOOL ON VACATION FOR THREE WEEKS IN JULY. DURING THE 15-DAY BREAKS, THE SCHOOL OFFERS SPECIAL PROGRAMS TO PROVIDE REMEDIAL OR ENRICHMENT CLASSES FOR ABOUT 150 STUDENTS.

TO MEET THE NEEDS OF ITS DIVERSE STUDENT POPULATION, EMERSON HAS DEVELOPED A SPECIAL FOCUS ON SCHOOL READINESS. IT OPERATES A CHILD DEVELOPMENT CENTER FOR ABOUT 40 PRESCHOOL CHILDREN (ONE OF SIX PROGRAMS IN ALBUQUERQUE). THE CENTER IS PARTICULARLY PROUD OF ITS EMPHASIS ON PARENT PARTICIPATION AND REPORTS HIGH RATES OF INVOLVEMENT IN PARENT WORKSHOPS AND MONTHLY PARENT-CHILD ACTIVITY DAYS.

ADDING SCHOOL REFORM TO THE LIST OF THINGS SCHOOLS MUST ACCOMPLISH, WITHOUT RECOGNIZING THAT TIME IS A FINITE RESOURCE SENDS A POWERFUL MESSAGE TO TEACHERS: DON'T TAKE THIS REFORM BUSINESS TOO SERIOUSLY. SQUEEZE IT IN ON YOUR OWN TIME.

- Resolution of the time issue "remains one of the most critical problems confronting educators today," according to the National Education Association. "For school employees involved in reform, time has become an implacable barrier."

As a representative of the American Federation of Teachers said at a recent Teachers Forum on GOALS 2000 sponsored by the U.S. Department of Education, "We've got to turn around the notion that we have to do everything without being given the time to do it."

Teachers, principals and administrators need *time* for reform. They need *time* to come up to speed as academic standards are overhauled, *time* to come to grips with new assessment systems, and *time* to make productive and effective use of greater professional autonomy, one hallmark of reform in the 1990s. Adding school reform to the list of things schools must accomplish, without recognizing that time in the current calendar is a limited resource, trivializes the effort. It sends a powerful message to teachers: don't take this reform business too seriously. Squeeze it in on your own time.

EMERGING CONTENT AND ACHIEVEMENT STANDARDS

As 1994 dawned, calls for much more demanding subject matter standards began

PROVIDING DAY CARE AND PRE-SCHOOL PROGRAMS
AMIDST RURAL POVERTY

LEADVILLE, COLORADO WAS IN TROUBLE WHEN JAMES MCCABE BECAME SUPERINTENDENT OF ITS LAKE COUNTY SCHOOLS (ENROLLING 1,100 STUDENTS IN A SMALL RURAL VALLEY OF ABOUT 5,000 RESIDENTS) IN 1987. THE COUNTY'S ECONOMIC BASE COLLAPSED WHEN A LOCAL MOLYBDENUM MINE SHUT DOWN, THROWING NEARLY 3,000 PEOPLE OUT OF WORK IN A ONE-COMPANY TOWN. FORCED TO DRIVE 45 MILES OR MORE TO FIND WORK AT HALF THE WAGES, LEADVILLE MEN AND WOMEN BEGAN OPERATING SKI-LIFTS, SELLING TICKETS AND SKI EQUIPMENT, AND CLEANING HOTEL ROOMS AT COLORADO'S RESORTS.

MCCABE'S SOLUTION WAS STRAIGHTFORWARD. COMBINE THE NEED FOR DAY CARE WITH THE EQUALLY PRESSING NEED FOR PRE-SCHOOL PREPARATION IN THIS LOW-INCOME COMMUNITY. ORGANIZING A COMMUNITY TEAM, HE PERSUADED THE SCHOOL DISTRICT TO TURN OVER AN ELEMENTARY SCHOOL WHICH WOULD BE USED FOR (1) AN AFFORDABLE PRE-SCHOOL PROGRAM FOR EVERY 2 1/2 TO 5 YEAR OLD CHILD IN THE COUNTY; (2) AFFORDABLE DAY CARE FOR ALL CHILDREN THROUGH AGE TEN 365 DAYS A YEAR (5:30 A.M. TO 6:30 P.M.); AND (3) BEFORE- AND AFTER-SCHOOL CARE FOR ALL 5 TO 13 YEAR OLDS IN THE COUNTY—ALL WITHOUT USING LOCAL PROPERTY TAX MONEY.

ACTIVITIES AT "THE CENTER" SNOWBALLED. ORIGINALLY INTENDED FOR PERHAPS 100 STUDENTS, THERE ARE NOW NEARLY 700 STUDENTS ENROLLED IN ALL OF ITS PROGRAMS. THE FACILITY'S ANNUAL BUDGET OF $600,000 IS FINANCED WITH FEDERAL, STATE, AND LOCAL GRANTS, PHILANTHROPIC CONTRIBUTIONS, AND MODEST FEES SCALED ON ABILITY TO PAY. ITS MOST IMPRESSIVE ACCOMPLISHMENT IS HELPING LOWER THE PROPORTION OF LOW-INCOME FAMILIES IN THE COUNTY BY FREEING PARENTS TO FIND WORK.

to bear fruit. Intended for all students, new content frameworks will extend across the school curriculum—English, science, history, geography, civics, the arts, foreign languages, and mathematics, among others. Their purpose is to bring all American youngsters up to world-class performance standards.

The American people and their educators need to be very clear about the standards movement. It is not time-free. At least three factors demand more time and better use of it.

First, subjects traditionally squeezed out of the curriculum now seek their place in the sun. Additional hours and days will be required if new standards in the arts, geography, and foreign languages are to be *even partially attained.*

Second, most students will find the traditional core curriculum significantly more demanding. Materials and concepts formerly reserved for the few must now be provided to the many. More student learning time and more flexible schedules for seminars, laboratories, team teaching, team learning, and homework will be essential.

Finally, one point cannot be restated too forcefully: professional development needs will be broad and massive. Indispensable to educated students are learned teachers in the classroom. An enormous change is at hand for the nation's 2.75 million teachers. To keep pace with changing content standards, teachers will need ongoing coursework in their disciplines *while they continue to teach their subjects.*

The Commission's hearings confirmed the time demands of the standards movement:

- **Arts.** "I am here to pound the table for 15 percent of school time devoted to arts instruction," declared Paul Lehman of the Consortium of National Arts Education Associations.

- **English.** "These standards will require a huge amount of time, for both students and teachers," Miles Myers of the

National Council of Teachers of English told the Commission.

- **Geography.** "Implementing our standards will require more time. Geography is hardly taught at all in American schools today," was the conclusion of Anthony De Souza of the National Geographic Society.

- **Mathematics.** "The standards I am describing are not the standards I received as a student or that I taught as a teacher," said James Gates of the National Council of Teachers of Mathematics.

- **Science.** "There is a consensus view that new standards will require more time," said David Florio of the National Academy of Sciences.

STRIKING THE SHACKLES OF TIME

Given the many demands made of schools today, the wonder is not that they do so poorly, but that they accomplish so much. Our society has stuffed additional burdens into the time envelope of 180 six-hour days without regard to the consequences for learning. We agree with the Maine mathematics teacher who said, "The problem with our schools is not that they are *not* what they used to be, but that they *are* what they used to be." In terms of time, our schools are unchanged despite a transformation in the world around them.

Each of the five issues - the design flaw, lack of academic time, out of school influences, time for educators, and new content and achievement standards - revolves around minutes, hours, and days. If the United States is to grasp the larger education ambitions for which it is reaching, we must strike the shackles of time from our schools.

LESSONS FROM ABROAD

International comparisons of education are difficult. Cultural factors influence performance and school systems differ. Despite such problems, international comparisons are not impossible and a great deal can be learned from examining schooling abroad. In fact, unflattering comparisons of the academic performance of American students with those from other lands spurred attempts at school improvement in the United States throughout the 1980s.

From its review of other nations, the Commission draws several conclusions:

- Students in other post-industrial democracies receive twice as much instruction in core academic areas during high school.

- Schools abroad protect academic time by distinguishing between the "academic day" and the "school day."

- Many of our economic competitors supplement formal education with significant out-of-school learning time.

- School performance abroad has consequences and is closely related to opportunities for employment and further education.

- Teachers in other countries enjoy freedom and respect as professionals.

In short, education abroad is built around high expectations. Schools hold themselves and the adults and students in them to high standards; in consequence they enjoy high levels of support from parents and the community. As the Commission observed first-hand, schools overseas reflect a cultural passion for learning.

AS 1994 DAWNED, CALLS FOR MUCH MORE DEMANDING SUBJECT MATTER STANDARDS BEGAN TO BEAR FRUIT. THEIR PURPOSE IS TO BRING ALL AMERICAN YOUNGSTERS UP TO WORLD-CLASS PERFORMANCE STANDARDS.

TWICE AS MUCH CORE INSTRUCTION

Recent comparisons of the number of annual "instructional hours" in different countries indicate that Americans rank in the top half of the nine countries examined. By the standard of time as an instructional resource, American education measures up well.

This standard, however, provides false comfort. As the Commission saw in Germany and Japan, learning is serious business abroad. "Academic time" is rarely touched. Distinctions are made between the academic day (which the Germans call the half day) and the school day (in Germany, the full day).

When asked about the school day, officials produce documents outlining a time frame similar to that in the typical American school. They feel no need to explain extracurricular activities within the school day, because these activities are not allowed to interfere with academic time. Academic time, by and large, is devoted to core academic study—native language and literature, mathematics, science, history, civics, geography, the arts, and second and third languages.

The use of "instructional" time in the United States is markedly different. The Commission analyzed time requirements for core academic subjects in 41 states and the District of Columbia.[1] The results are startling: on average, students can receive a high school diploma—often sufficient in itself for university entrance—if they devote only 41 percent of their school time to core academic work.

It is conceivable that American students devote more time to demanding coursework than states require. That hope, however, is misplaced: 1993 data from the U.S. Department of Education indicate that the

---

1 Nine states did not provide information.

FIGURE 1[2]

THE FINAL FOUR YEARS IN FOUR NATIONS:
ESTIMATED REQUIRED CORE ACADEMIC TIME

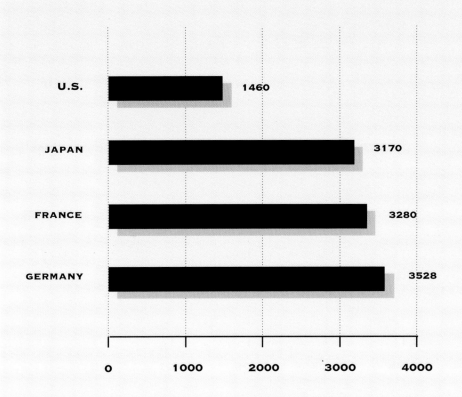

TOTAL HOURS REQUIRED

2 Sources: United States estimate developed from The Digest of Education Statistics (NCES, 1992), State Education Indicators (Council of Chief State School Officers, 1990), and the Commission's review of academic requirements in 41 states and the District of Columbia. The estimate for Japan was developed from Monbusho (1993 publication of the Japanese Ministry of Education, Science and Culture) and site visits to Japanese secondary schools, and confirmed by senior Japanese ministry officials at a meeting in Washington. The estimate for France was developed from a French publication, Organization of the French Educational System Leading to the French Baccalaureat, and confirmed by French officials. The German estimate is actually the number of hours of required coursework for one state, Berlin.

course of study most students follow is very close to what states require.

Figure 1 compares requirements for core academic instruction in the final four years of secondary school in four countries: Germany, France, Japan, and the United States. It displays minimum time requirements at the secondary level in core academic subjects, based on our observations abroad and official state and national publications. In their final four years of secondary school, according to our estimates, French, German, and Japanese students receive more than twice as much core academic instruction as American students. Although these estimates are approximations, we are convinced they reflect the magnitude of the academic time trap in which American schools are caught.

Figure 1 speaks for itself. No matter how the assumptions underlying the figure are modified, the result is always the same—students abroad are required to work on demanding subject matter at least twice as long. In practical terms, this means that most foreign students are studying language, literature, science and two or more languages, while many of our young people spend their time in study halls, pep rallies, driver education, and assemblies.

Even the most committed advocate of the *status quo* will concede that American students cannot learn as much as their foreign peers in half the time. By this standard, our education system still has a long way to go.

One need look no further than Figure 1 to understand why European and Asian visitors to the United States commonly understand English while their children outperform American students on tests of student achievement. Americans abroad, by contrast, assume they will deal with people who speak English. Our high school students have trouble reading, writing, and solving simple mathematics problems.

The emphasis on core academic instruction abroad does not mean that other activities are ignored. Up to 50 percent of German students, even in farming areas, remain at the school after the academic day to participate in clubs, sports, and additional classes of one kind or another. In Japan, students clean their school when the academic day ends and then enter activity periods.

OUT-OF-SCHOOL LEARNING

The formidable learning advantage Japanese and German schools provide to their students is complemented by equally impressive out-of-school learning. Large numbers of Japanese students (two-thirds of all students in Tokyo; nationally about 15 percent of all students in grade four rising to nearly 50 percent by grade nine) attend jukus—private, tutorial services that enrich instruction, provide remedial help, and prepare students for university examinations.

A Japanese research institute official told the Commission that elementary school teachers teach to the "middle of the class." Gifted students who might get bored or students who need extra assistance are expected to turn to the juku for help.

Jukus are a big business in Japan. Spending on the estimated 35,000 jukus reaches about 800 billion yen annually (over $7 billion), costing the average family, according to Japanese officials, about $2,500 per year, per child.

In Japan, schools and the larger society generally ignore "ability" or "aptitude" as factors in school success. The Japanese are convinced that hard work can help every student meet high standards. Diligence, application, and enterprise are the keys—if a student is not "getting it," more time, usually self-directed time, is the answer.

Jukus do not exist in Germany. But if German students are similar to their peers throughout Europe, 50 percent of them spend two or more hours on daily homework, and only 7 or 8 percent watch television for five or more hours a day. In the United States, only 29 percent of students report doing as much homework and three times as many watch television daily for five or more hours.

In sum, compared to American students, German and Japanese youth are exposed in high school to much more demanding academic subjects, for many more hours.

They spend more serious time learning out-side the school. And they fritter away less time in front of the television.

PERFORMANCE CARRIES CONSEQUENCES

Another distinction that can be drawn between American education and schooling abroad is in consequences for school perfor-mance. In Germany and Japan, learning matters. Performance, not seat time, is what counts. Students understand that what they learn in school will make a real difference to their chances in life. In the United States, paper credentials count. Apart from the small percentage of students interested in highly selective colleges and universities, most students understand that possession of even a mediocre high school diploma is enough to get them into some kind of college or job.

Students in German vocational schools know that what they learn in class is closely related to what they will do on the job, because their apprenticeship experience (an alternating routine of learning in class and learning on the job) demonstrates the rela-tionship every day. German students inter-ested in pursuing a university career also understand that they will have to pass the *Abitur*, a demanding examination covering secondary school preparation.

Examination pressure is even more severe in Japan. Since attendance in upper sec-ondary schools (grades 10-12) is not com-pulsory in Japan, young people take exami-nations even to enter public high schools. Although 90 percent of Japanese young people complete high school, the particular high school attended is critical to the chances for university admission. Moreover, Japanese students also must sit for intense, pressure-filled, competitive examinations for admission to the best uni-versities.

PROFESSIONAL PRACTICE

Teachers are held to much higher stan-dards in both Germany and Japan. In Germany, teachers are expected to be more

knowledgeable in their subjects than are teachers in the United States. Teacher preparation, consequently, takes up to six years (compared to four in the United States). In Japan, aspiring teachers are required to pass a rigorous examination prior to certification. The organization of school time in both societies encourages continued development of teachers, who are given the time they need to grow and cooperate as professionals.

Japanese teachers generally deal with more students in each classroom, but teach fewer classes; the typical class has between 35 and 40 students, compared to an average of 23 in the United States. However, Japanese teachers are typically in "front of the class" for only four hours a day. Time spent outside the classroom is not considered wasted, but an essential aspect of professional work. The same phenomenon can be seen in Germany—teachers are in front of a class for 21 to 24 hours a week, but their work week is 38 hours long. Non-classroom time is spent on preparation, grading, in-service education, and consulting with colleagues.

In both countries, the Commission sensed considerably greater encouragement of teacher professionalism than is apparent in the United States. In Germany, for example, teachers select the texts they will use to meet *Länder* (state) standards; in 15 of the 16 states, teachers design and administer their own tests for the *Abitur*, and teachers validate colleagues' testing by sharing examinations with each other and discussing test questions.

NOT JUST A MATTER OF TIME

It is clear from these observations that the issue of improving student performance is not simply a matter of time. Time is clearly critical. In the context of a global market for educated people, the fact that youth abroad receive the equivalent of several additional years of schooling cannot be ignored. But other factors are equally important. Elsewhere, core academic instruction is emphasized. Academic time

is protected. Expectations for out-of-school learning are high. Teachers are held to high standards and treated as professionals.

All of these are critical factors in the success of schooling abroad. And all of them are feasible, because foreign schools understand that effective learning depends on freeing schools, teachers, and students from the bonds of time.

RECOMMENDATIONS

As various panaceas have been advanced in the last decade to solve the problems of learning in America, education reform has moved in fits and starts. Indeed, as different helmsmen have seized the wheel, the ship of education reform has gone round in circles. If we have learned anything from these efforts, it is that no single solution exists for the problems of American schools.

Reform can only succeed if it is broad and comprehensive, attacking many problems simultaneously. In that effort, high standards and time are more than simply additional oars in the water. With standards as our compass, time can be the rudder of reform.

In our judgment, educators have created a false dilemma in debating whether additional instructional time can be found within the confines of the current day and calendar, or needs to be sought by extending both. False dilemmas produce bad choices. To meet new demands, the United States needs both—the best use of available time and more time.

EIGHT RECOMMENDATIONS

We offer eight recommendations to put time at the top of the nation's reform agenda:

I.   **REINVENT SCHOOLS AROUND LEARNING, NOT TIME.**

II.   **FIX THE DESIGN FLAW: USE TIME IN NEW AND BETTER WAYS.**

III.   **ESTABLISH AN ACADEMIC DAY.**

IV.   **KEEP SCHOOLS OPEN LONGER TO MEET THE NEEDS OF CHILDREN AND COMMUNITIES.**

V.   **GIVE TEACHERS THE TIME THEY NEED.**

VI.   **INVEST IN TECHNOLOGY.**

VII.   **DEVELOP LOCAL ACTION PLANS TO TRANSFORM SCHOOLS.**

VIII.   **SHARE THE RESPONSIBILITY: FINGER POINTING AND EVASION MUST END.**

VETERAN TEACHERS ARE WELL AWARE THAT TODAY'S STUDENTS BRING MANY MORE PROBLEMS TO SCHOOL THAN CHILDREN DID A GENERATION AGO.

I.

REINVENT SCHOOLS AROUND LEARNING, NOT TIME

WE RECOMMEND A COMMITMENT TO BRING EVERY CHILD IN THE UNITED STATES TO WORLD-CLASS STANDARDS IN CORE ACADEMIC AREAS.

By far the most important part of this Commission's charge relates not to time but to student learning. The first issue is not "How much time is enough?" but "What are we trying to accomplish?" As witnesses repeatedly told the Commission, there is no point to adding more time to today's schools if it is used in the same way. We must use time in new, different, and better ways.

The Commission is convinced the following areas represent the common core all students should master: English and language arts, mathematics, science, civics, history, geography, the arts, and foreign languages. This core defines a set of expectations students abroad are routinely expected to meet. American students can meet them as well.

Regular assessments at different stages of students' lives should require every student to demonstrate a firm grasp of demanding material in each of these areas, a grasp extending far beyond the trivial demands of most multiple-choice tests. They should assess not only the mastery of essential facts, but also the student's ability to write, reason, and analyze.

II.

FIX THE DESIGN FLAW: USE TIME IN NEW AND BETTER WAYS

WE RECOMMEND THAT STATE AND LOCAL BOARDS WORK WITH SCHOOLS
TO REDESIGN EDUCATION SO THAT TIME BECOMES A FACTOR SUPPORTING LEARNING,
NOT A BOUNDARY MARKING ITS LIMITS.

The conviction that learning goals should be fixed and time a flexible resource opens up profound opportunities for change.

At a minimum, fixing the design flaw means recognizing that very young children enter school at very different levels of readiness. Some enter kindergarten already reading. Others readily manage computer programs appropriate to their age and skill levels. But some cannot recognize letters from the alphabet or identify numbers or pictures. Sadly, too many are already abused and neglected. School readiness is the basic foundation on which the rest of the school program is built.

Fixing the design flaw also makes possible radical change in the teaching and learning process. New uses of time should ensure that schools rely much less on the 51-minute period, after which teachers and students drop everything to rush off to the next class. Block scheduling—the use of two or more periods for extended exploration of complex topics or for science laboratories—should become more common. Providing a more flexible school day could also permit American schools to follow international practice—between classes students remain in the room and teachers come to them.

A more flexible time schedule is likely to encourage greater use of team teaching, in which groups of teachers, often from different disciplines, work together with students. Greater flexibility in the schedule will also make it easier for schools to take advantage of instructional resources in the community—workplaces, libraries, churches, and community youth groups—and to work effectively with emerging technologies.

Fixing the design flaw means that grouping children by age should become a thing of the past. It makes no more sense to put a computer-literate second grader in *Introduction to Computers* than it does to place a recent Hispanic immigrant in *Introductory Spanish*. Both should be placed at their level of accomplishment. Although the Commission does not believe 15-year olds should leave high school early, meeting high performance standards in key subjects should be the requirement for the high school diploma, not simply seat time or Carnegie units. In the case of genuinely exceptional students who meet these requirements while very young, schools should offer them the opportunity to take advanced courses.

Above all, fixing the flaw means that time should be adjusted to meet the individual needs of learners, rather than the administrative convenience of adults. The dimensions of time in the learning process extend far beyond whether one student needs more time and another can do with less. The flexible use of time can permit more individualized instruction.

We should not forget that students are like adults in many ways. Some are able to focus intensely on demanding materials for long periods; others need more frequent breaks. Many students, like many adults, learn best by reading; some learn best by listening; others, by doing, or even by talking amongst themselves. Offering more frequent breaks, providing more opportunities for hands-on learning, encouraging group work—these techniques and others can parole some of the students who today feel most confined by the school's rigid time demands.

All of these possibilities—and many others—lie within reach if the design flaw is fixed. All of them are much more difficult within the prison of time-bound education.

31

III.

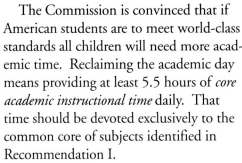

ESTABLISH AN ACADEMIC DAY

WE RECOMMEND THAT SCHOOLS PROVIDE ADDITIONAL ACADEMIC TIME BY RECLAIMING THE SCHOOL DAY FOR ACADEMIC INSTRUCTION.

The Commission is convinced that if American students are to meet world-class standards all children will need more academic time. Reclaiming the academic day means providing at least 5.5 hours of *core academic instructional time* daily. That time should be devoted exclusively to the common core of subjects identified in Recommendation I.

The Commission's analysis of how time is currently used in American schools makes one thing clear: even within the confines of a 180-day school year, reclaiming the academic day should, alone, nearly double the amount of instructional time in core curriculum areas. For some students, reclaiming the academic day will provide all the additional time they need to meet new standards. For most others, however, more academic time will be required.

Establishing an academic day means, in essence, that the existing school day be devoted almost exclusively to core academic instruction. What this means is obvious: many worthwhile student programs—athletics, clubs, and other activities—will have to be sacrificed unless the school day is lengthened. We do not believe they should be sacrificed, or that communities will agree to do without them. At the same time, we cannot agree to sacrificing the academic core of the school to other activities. Instead, all student activities should be offered during a longer school day.

Compensatory programs and special efforts for the gifted and talented can be provided during the longer school day. Language instruction for non-native English speakers should be provided in this longer day. Students who want to accelerate their studies, perhaps spending only three years in high school, can also use this time.

IS THERE A BETTER WAY?

DEVELOPING A NEW GENERATION OF SCIENTISTS, SCHOLARS, AND LEADERS

No one can visit the Thomas Jefferson High School for Science and Technology, Alexandria, Virginia, without realizing it is one of the most remarkable public schools in the United States—remarkable for the wealth of the suburban school district that supports it, the talents of its selected students, the skill of its staff, the technologies it employs, and the support it receives from the business community.

It is remarkable for something else as well. Its schedule is different; every school day at Thomas Jefferson is lengthened by one period, during which every one of its 1,600 9th to 12th graders is required to participate in a student activity or related coursework such as tutoring, laboratories, or guidance activities. Daily schedules are also flexible enough to let every class meet for at least one double-period every week.

The selectivity of the school—and corporate sponsorship of state-of-the-art technological environments in areas such as optics, energy systems, telecommunications, biotechnology, and industrial robotics—makes it easy to overlook the school's schedule as a factor in its success.

What does the extra period mean in practice? According to sophomore Paul Helms, "It is one of the most important things in the school. I use it to go to both the Fellowship of Christian Athletes and to a Latin Honors class." Senior Seth Mitcho: "Eighth period has helped make this school the center of our lives and often of our families."

A schedule that helps make school the center of the lives of students and families may be the most remarkable thing about the Thomas Jefferson High School for Science and Technology.

IV.

KEEP SCHOOLS OPEN LONGER TO MEET THE NEEDS OF CHILDREN AND COMMUNITIES

WE RECOMMEND THAT SCHOOLS RESPOND TO THE NEEDS OF TODAY'S STUDENTS BY REMAINING OPEN LONGER DURING THE DAY AND THAT SOME SCHOOLS IN EVERY DISTRICT REMAIN OPEN THROUGHOUT THE YEAR.

No magic number of hours in the day, or days in the year, will guarantee learning for all students. As a rule of thumb, about 5.5 hours of core academic instruction daily is a useful frame of reference for the typical student. But it is only a frame of reference. Many students will need more time; some will need less.

As noted under Recommendation III, establishing an academic day of necessity requires lengthening the school day, both for extracurricular activities and for time to offer some students academic programs designed to give them special help or opportunities.

Schools open throughout the year can also provide many services to adults, serving as centers in which community agencies offer adult education, "intergenerational" literacy efforts teaching parents and children together, and programs stressing, for example, parenting or job skills. When the walls of the prison of time are torn down, schools can realize their full potential as community learning centers, vibrant and responsive to the educational needs of citizens of every age.

We stress again that many children, in many different communities, are growing up today without the family and community support taken for granted when the public school was created 150 years ago. The documented need for child care and uncoordinated nature of the variety of public and private providers now trying to meet it—licensed and unlicensed, for profit and not-for-profit, in homes and in community facilities—can no longer be ignored.

No single agency can meet all of the needs of today's families, nor can any major public agency ignore them. Extended-day services that offer safe havens for children in troubled neighborhoods are a logical solution to the child care problem; a problem that does not go away when schools close for the summer. Moreover, schools have every interest in making sure that a wide variety of other services—immunizations, health screening, nutrition, and mental health, among others—are available to children and their families. Without such services, it is unlikely that the first of the National Education Goals ("school readiness") can be achieved.

Fixing the design flaw requires acknowledging something else as well: state mandatory attendance requirements defining how many days students should attend school should not define how many days schools should remain open. In fact, state financial support should encourage more learning time. If Americans are ever to escape the education time trap, some schools in every district should be open throughout the year so that students can find the help they need, when they need it.

Finally, we note that in suggesting greater use of school facilities to meet the needs of children and communities, we are not recommending that schools provide these services directly or pay for them. Schools should act as advocates, insisting that the needs of children and families be met and making school facilities available whenever possible for services essential to student learning.

IS THERE A BETTER WAY?

THE EXTENDED DAY AND YEAR: ONE COMMUNITY'S EXPERIENCE WITH PUBLIC DEMAND

THE MURFREESBORO SCHOOLS IN TENNESSEE MAY HAVE THE MOST COMPREHENSIVE EXTENDED-DAY AND -YEAR PROGRAM IN THE UNITED STATES. IN 1986, MURFREESBORO DECIDED THAT COMMUNITY CONCERN ABOUT LATCH-KEY CHILDREN WAS STRONG ENOUGH TO JUSTIFY EXTENDING THE SCHOOL YEAR. THE DISTRICT ANNOUNCED THAT ONE ELEMENTARY SCHOOL WOULD BE OPEN FROM 6:00 A.M. UNTIL 6:00 P.M. WITH PARENTS PAYING FOR THE EXTENDED-DAY SERVICES. FOUR STUDENTS SHOWED UP. WITHIN TWO YEARS, PUBLIC DEMAND FORCED THE EXTENSION OF THE CONCEPT TO EVERY ELEMENTARY SCHOOL IN THE CITY. THIS YEAR, 50 PERCENT OF THE CITY'S 5,000 ELEMENTARY SCHOOL STUDENTS CAN BE FOUND IN THE PROGRAM ON ANY GIVEN DAY, ALL ON A VOLUNTARY BASIS ON THE PART OF PARENTS.

PLANS ARE NOW WELL ADVANCED TO OPEN MURFREESBORO'S FIRST K-8 YEAR-ROUND SCHOOL IN AUGUST 1994. PARENTAL FREEDOM OF CHOICE WILL DETERMINE ENROLLMENT. DISTINGUISHING BETWEEN THE "SCHOOL DAY," "EDUCATIONAL SERVICES," AND "EXTENDED SCHOOL SERVICES," THE SCHOOL WILL OFFER EDUCATIONAL SERVICES FROM 8:00 A.M. UNTIL 5:30 P.M., AND EXTENDED SERVICES BEFORE SCHOOL FROM 6:00 A.M. AND AFTER SCHOOL UNTIL 7:00 P.M. EXTENDED SERVICES WILL BE AVAILABLE FIVE DAYS A WEEK, 52 WEEKS A YEAR. INTERIM SESSIONS WILL OFFER 40 EXTRA DAYS OF ACADEMIC TIME.

PARENTS CHOOSING TO TAKE ADVANTAGE OF EDUCATIONAL SERVICES FOR THEIR CHILDREN AFTER 3:00 P.M. (OR DURING THE 40 DAYS) WILL PAY A SMALL FEE, AS WILL PARENTS OPTING FOR EXTENDED SERVICES. STUDENTS DIRECTED BY SCHOOL PERSONNEL TO ATTEND SUPPLEMENTARY CLASSES WILL DO SO AT DISTRICT EXPENSE. MURFREESBORO EXPECTS TO ACCOMPLISH ALL OF THIS WITHIN ITS REGULAR PER-PUPIL EXPENDITURES FIGURES. MAYOR JOE JACKSON BRIDLES AT THE SUGGESTION THAT EXTENDED SERVICES UNDERMINE THE FAMILY: "YOU'VE GOT IT EXACTLY BACKWARDS," HE RESPONDS. "THESE SERVICES SUPPORT THE FAMILY BY MAKING IT POSSIBLE FOR PEOPLE TO WORK WITHOUT WORRYING BECAUSE THEY KNOW THEIR CHILDREN ARE INVOLVED IN CONSTRUCTIVE LEARNING."

V.

GIVE TEACHERS THE TIME
THEY NEED

WE RECOMMEND THAT TEACHERS BE
PROVIDED WITH THE PROFESSIONAL
TIME AND OPPORTUNITIES THEY NEED
TO DO THEIR JOBS.

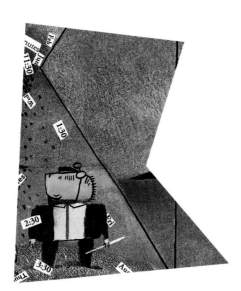

The daily working life of most teachers is one of unrelieved time pressure and isolation; they work, largely alone, in a classroom of 25-30 children or adolescents for hours every day. Unlike teachers in many systems overseas, who can take advantage of continuous, daily opportunities for professional development, American teachers have little time for preparation, planning, cooperation, or professional growth.

The Commission believes that time for planning and professional development is urgently needed—not as a frill or an add-on, but as a major aspect of the agreement between teachers and districts.

The whole question of teachers and time needs to be rethought in a serious and systematic way. The issue is not simply teachers. It is not just time. The real issue is education quality. Teachers need time to develop effective lessons. They need time to assess students in meaningful ways and discuss the results with students individually. They need time to talk to students, and listen to them, and to confer with parents and other family members. They need time to read professional journals, interact with their colleagues, and watch outstanding teachers demonstrate new strategies.

Districts can provide this time in several ways: extending the contract year to pay teachers for professional development, using the longer day for the same purpose, or providing for the widespread and systematic use of a cadre of well-prepared, full-time, substitute teachers.

The last thing districts should encourage is sending children home to provide time for "teacher professional days." We will never have truly effective schools while teachers' needs are met at the expense of students' learning time.

VI.

INVEST IN TECHNOLOGY

WE RECOMMEND THAT SCHOOLS SEIZE ON THE PROMISE OF
NEW TECHNOLOGIES TO INCREASE PRODUCTIVITY, ENHANCE STUDENT ACHIEVEMENT,
AND EXPAND LEARNING TIME.

Technology is a great unrealized hope in education reform. It can transform learning by improving both the effectiveness of existing time and making more time available through self-guided instruction, both in school and out. Technology has already changed much of the rest of American society—profit and non-profit, private sector and government alike—because it makes it possible to produce more with less. A similar revolution is possible in education.

At a minimum, computers and other technological aids promise to rid teachers and administrators of the mundane record keeping that is such a characteristic of school life today, permitting teachers to spend more time designing instructional programs for their students.

But the true promise of technology lies in the classroom. Technology makes it possible for today's schools to escape the assembly-line mentality of the "factory model" school. With emerging hardware and software, educators can personalize learning.

Instead of the lock-step of lecture and laboratory, computers and other new telecommunications technologies make it possible for students to move at their own pace. Effective learning technologies have already demonstrated their ability to pique student interest and increase motivation, encouraging students not only to spend more of their own time in learning but also to be more deeply involved in what they are doing.

Finally, it should be noted that the "information superhighway" can reshape education as it will other areas of American life. The school revolution, however, depends both on a concerted investment strategy to help educators obtain these technologies and on educators confronting their reluctance to supplement the techniques of the 19th century (textbooks, chalk and blackboards) with the technologies of the 21st (CD-ROMs, modems, and fiber optics). They must do so. In order to help them, states should establish special funds to provide low-interest loans and grants, and they should create large-scale purchasing agreements for new technologies and teacher training in their use.

VII.

DEVELOP LOCAL ACTION PLANS TO TRANSFORM SCHOOLS

WE RECOMMEND THAT EVERY DISTRICT CONVENE LOCAL LEADERS TO DEVELOP
ACTION PLANS THAT OFFER DIFFERENT SCHOOL OPTIONS AND ENCOURAGE PARENTS,
STUDENTS, AND TEACHERS TO CHOOSE AMONG THEM.

School reform cannot work if it is imposed on the community top-down. Genuine, long-lasting reform grows from the grassroots.

The Commission believes every community must engage in a community-wide debate about the shape and future of its schools. To that end, we encourage every district, with the support of the superintendent and local school board, to engage major school stakeholders in a comprehensive, long-term dialogue about the hopes, aspirations, and future directions of local education. The conversation should include students, parents, taxpayers, employers, and representatives of public assistance, juvenile justice, health and other social services agencies. It should be organized around learning time. If this conversation is to be productive, it is essential to include teachers and administrators as equal partners.

We are convinced that larger school districts can offer families a wide array of alternative school calendars by encouraging individual schools to adopt distinctive approaches. The more options, the better. No single configuration will satisfy every need. Districts of any size, with a sense of vision, boldness, and entrepreneurship can experiment with block scheduling, team teaching, longer days and years, and extending time with new distance-learning technologies.

No community in the United States is so small or impoverished that it cannot benefit from an examination of how it uses time—

if not in extending the day or year, at least in re-configuring how it uses the time now available.

The Commission wants to stress that this recommendation provides a real opportunity for local leadership groups—the business community, colleges and universities, churches, civic groups, newspapers and the electronic media—to go beyond criticizing schools by helping frame the education debate community by community. This is not just a task for educators. There can be no doubt that the 1989 Education Summit, convened under the leadership of the White House and the nation's governors, went a long way towards focusing Americans on the goals they hold in common for their schools. Local leaders can do a lot to transform their communities and their schools by convening similar education summits, county by county, city by city, district by district, and, if need be, school by school.

Finally, the Commission issues a challenge to local school boards: use your time to perform the leadership role for which you have been elected or appointed.

Recent analyses demonstrate convincingly that far too many boards function as managers instead of policymakers. School board time should be devoted to local policy, goals, and the education needs of children, not to micro-management of school operations.

Our challenge: help your community crystallize a vision for its schools.

"YEAR-ROUND EDUCATION"

PRINCIPAL HOWARD LAPPIN OF LOS ANGELES' JAMES A. FOSHAY MIDDLE SCHOOL SHOWED THE COMMISSION AN EXAMPLE OF A "YEAR-ROUND EDUCATION" PROGRAM. DESPITE THE NAME, MOST YEAR-ROUND SCHOOLS ARE A REORGANIZATION OF THE 180-DAY SCHOOL YEAR; THEY DO NOT PROVIDE ADDITIONAL TIME FOR EITHER LEARNING OR NONACADEMIC SERVICES. NEVERTHELESS, THEIR EXISTENCE INDICATES THAT ALTERNATIVE CALENDARS ARE FEASIBLE IN MANY AREAS AND YEAR-ROUND EDUCATION IS PROBABLY THE MOST WIDELY COPIED ALTERNATIVE TO THE TRADITIONAL CALENDAR. NATIONWIDE, NEARLY 2,000 PUBLIC AND PRIVATE SCHOOLS, ENROLLING MORE THAN 1.4 MILLION CHILDREN, ARE ON YEAR-ROUND CALENDARS, WITH THE LION'S SHARE OF SCHOOLS AND ENROLLMENT IN CALIFORNIA—ABOUT 1,300 SCHOOLS AND 1.16 MILLION CHILDREN.

THE YEAR-ROUND SCHEDULE CREATES FOUR SEPARATE SCHOOLS WITHIN FOSHAY'S WALLS. FOSHAY OPERATES FOUR DIFFERENT SCHEDULES, EACH BEGINNING AND ENDING AT A DIFFERENT TIME OF THE YEAR WITH ONE QUARTER OF THE SCHOOL'S ENROLLMENT. STUDENTS NORMALLY SPEND ONLY 180 DAYS AT SCHOOL, BUT IT IS USED YEAR ROUND, WITH THREE-QUARTERS OF THE SCHOOL'S ENROLLMENT IN THE BUILDING AT ANY GIVEN TIME. TWO-WEEK INTER-SESSIONS BETWEEN SCHOOL TERMS PERMIT STUDENTS TO RECEIVE AN ADDITIONAL 60 HOURS (TEN DAYS) OF INSTRUCTION IF NEEDED.

THE SCHOOL OPERATES SOME SATURDAY CLASSES FOR BOTH STUDENTS AND PARENTS, INCLUDING A JOINT EFFORT WITH THE UNIVERSITY OF SOUTHERN CALIFORNIA. THE JOINT PROGRAM ENROLLS 60 STUDENTS WHO ARE GUARANTEED FULL ASSISTANCE TO ATTEND USC IF THEY PERSIST AND COMPLETE THE SCHOLASTIC ASSESSMENT TEST WITH COMBINED MATH AND ENGLISH SCORES OF AT LEAST 1000. THE USC PROGRAM ALSO REQUIRES MANDATORY SATURDAY CLASSES FOR THE STUDENTS AND THEIR PARENTS.

VIII.

WE RECOMMEND THAT ALL OF OUR PEOPLE SHOULDER THEIR INDIVIDUAL
RESPONSIBILITIES TO TRANSFORM LEARNING IN AMERICA.

No single recommendation can capture the essential point with which the Commission concluded the first chapter: learning must become a national obsession in the United States.

In America's great education debate we find too often a belief that the solution is up to government or "the system." Nothing could be further from the truth. It is up to us. Most of what needs to be done can only be done by the people most directly involved. There are no short-cuts. Lightning will not strike and transform American schools if each of us acts as though the task belongs to somebody else.

To put learning in America powerfully back on track everyone will have to do more, make sacrifices, and work harder. Great institutions like the American school do not fail simply because they collapse from within. Complacency within combines with public apathy to enfeeble institutions, leaving behind impressive but empty facades.

The implications are clear. Schools cannot do the job alone. All of us have to shoulder our responsibilities. If we think this transformation too difficult, we must again learn the wisdom of the African proverb, "It takes a whole village to raise a child."

It takes a family to raise a child. Parents are more than their children's "first teachers"—they are lifelong examples bearing witness to community norms and expectations, to the values that give meaning, texture, and a sense of purpose to life.

It takes communities to raise a child. But in place of healthy communities, too often we find neighborhoods deteriorating amidst the alienation, rootlessness, and despair of violent streets.

It takes schools to raise a child. But where there should be a shared sense of common purpose among school, family, and community, too often we find a circle of blame. Parents blame the community for the child's problems. Communities blame the school. And the school, too frequently, blames both. Then it closes itself off in its time-bound world.

The finger pointing and evasions must come to an end—up and down the line from the federal government to the family and student. Although concrete recommendations are difficult to make, several ground rules point the way ahead.

Government should focus on results, not red tape. The sheer number of rules and regulations hamstringing schools from federal and state governments has grown beyond reason. Their cumulative effect is to handcuff schools.

All federal programs should follow the larger intent of the Clinton administration's legislation, *GOALS 2000: Educate America Act.* This bipartisan legislation puts the National Education Goals into statutory language. It promises to free local schools from regulation in favor of accountability. It focuses on results, not red tape.

The federal government should encourage local schools to use categorical programs to supplement *learning time* for target students. Too often these programs have defeated their own purpose: funds have been used for programs that replace the school's learning time. They should support after-school, weekend, and summer programs.

At the state level, the Commission applauds states such as Kentucky and Washington which have adopted comprehensive education reform efforts, most of which promise to (1) limit regulatory oversight in return for demonstrated results in the schools; (2) offer additional time for teachers' professional development; and (3) provide sanctions and rewards for schools based on performance.

It is at the school district and local board level that we find the major possibilities for freeing schools of red tape in favor of accountability. A large number of promising experiments are underway around the country to free schools of burdensome district regulation. Many of these experiments revolve around time; many do not. We encourage school boards—through the local action plans suggested in Recommendation VII—to examine these experiments and adapt the most promising to their own needs.

Higher education needs to get involved. Colleges and universities, as institutions, have been bystanders for the most part in the school reform debate. It is time they got involved. They can help in at least four ways.

First, higher education already offers a model that holds learning fixed and makes time a variable. Students can earn a bachelor's degree in three, four, even eight years; the same is true of doctoral study.

Second, the school reform movement *cannot* succeed unless academic institutions honor the results of new standards and assessments. Admissions requirements should validate learning, not seat time.

Third, colleges and universities educating teachers must align their programs with the movement to higher standards. This will involve changing not only offerings in schools of education, but also the design of undergraduate programs in core disciplines.

Finally, a handful of colleges and universities across the country are struggling to reinvent local schools. There are 3,500 colleges and universities in the United States and there should be 3,500 examples. It is not necessary to operate a school or district or provide medical checkups and family counseling—although some academic institutions are doing each of these things. But it is necessary to do something.

The business world should keep up the pressure. Much of the impetus for school reform, at the national, state, and local levels, has been generated by business leaders insisting that changes in the workplace require radically different kinds of school graduates. Corporate and small business leaders have also been actively supporting reform coalitions, applying corporate techniques to school operations, and creating a variety of one-on-one school partnerships in which individual firms work directly with individual classrooms, schools, or districts.

Now is no time for timidity in the school reform effort. Leaders cannot blow an uncertain trumpet. Business leaders must keep up the pressure for comprehensive reform to improve student achievement.

Parents, students, and teachers must lead the way. Finally, we want to speak directly to the people with the greatest stake in the learning enterprise—parents, grandparents, aunts, uncles, foster parents and guardians, and to teachers and students themselves.

To parents, grandparents, relatives and guardians: With your support for the agenda for reform outlined in this document, success is assured. Without it, we do not know how the agenda can be achieved.

You may worry that new academic standards will add to your children's stress. That is not our intent. In fact, that is why we insist that time be made a part of the standards discussion. Indeed, our hope is that schools will be more attractive, interesting, and lively places for both students and adults when time becomes the servant of learning. Schools should also be more hospitable to you, once teachers are released from the relentless treadmill of today's calendar and the academic day is more attuned to your family's needs.

We know that your aspirations for your children are unlimited, no matter your circumstances or the difficulties in which you find yourselves. You can bring those aspirations within reach. We have little to offer other than the advice of experts. But their words bear repeating. Play with your children every day. Read to them every night. Make sure they see a doctor regularly. Take an active interest in the day-to-day activities of the school and the community. Check homework, turn off the television, and make sure that your teenagers are not working so long earning pocket money that they have no time for school. Above all, encourage your children.

What we ask, of course, takes time. But your reward will come as you watch your children become the kind of men and women you knew they could be.

To teachers: You are the inheritors of a tradition of service and scholarship stretching back through history. Your first obligation is to that inheritance.

If you accept minimal effort from students or colleagues or excuse shoddy performance, then you have fallen short, no matter how understandable your reasons. You cannot remain true to the tradition you bear by acquiescing to the social promotion of students who are not prepared for the next step.

Only parents and students have a greater stake than you in this debate. Clearly our proposals will make a huge difference in your working life. The nature of the change, however, remains to be worked out with your participation. This Commission consciously avoided specifying a precise number of days in the school year, or hours in the school day, because we believe those issues must be worked out district by district and school by school.

Although we insist on breaking down the prison walls, it is not our intention to impose new demands on you without providing the support we know you need. It is up to you and your colleagues to put muscle and sinew on the reform framework outlined in this document. We think you will—not because we recommend it, but because you know it is right. You best understand that we are correct when we say learning is a prisoner of time.

Your satisfaction will lie in a more professional working environment. It will also be found in a lifetime following the progress of adults who achieved their full potential because of what you were able to do with and for them in the classroom.

Last, we say to students: We know that in the midst of today's pressures, your classes,

school, and homework often appear to be distractions from the business of growing up. We were once in your shoes. We, however, were lucky. When we left school, we expected to face a promising future, and for the most part our expectations were met.

You, too, can make good if you are prepared to work at it. You may think your academic success depends on whether or not you are "smart." But academic progress, as our international friends understand, depends on hard work and perseverance. It is your job to learn, to become the "worker" in your own education. You must understand that learning is never a passive activity; it is always active. Your success in school depends primarily on your own diligence. The returns on your efforts will be many, including the satisfaction of knowing that adults who complained about your generation were wrong—and you proved them wrong.

FINANCING: DOLLARS, SCHOLARS, AND TIME

"Time is money," runs an old adage. There is no doubt that the recommendations we have advanced will cost money. We suggest it will be money well spent. In fact, a leading economist suggests that when we consider the costs of day care, the effects of summer learning loss, and the ultimate benefits of increased learning time, we can view any initial costs for such time as an investment with more promising pay-offs than most other uses of tax dollars. Where are the funds to come from in a period in which the federal domestic budget is frozen for the next several years, state revenues and outlays are under pressure, and local taxpayers resist higher taxes? The picture in public finance is not optimistic.

But neither is it a disaster. The United States is the wealthiest country in the history of the world. American schools are already handsomely supported by international standards. In constant, inflation-adjusted dollars, real spending on education in America increased 200 percent between 1959 and 1989-90.

We are convinced the American people will support these recommendations if they believe high quality education will accompany the changes and if educators bring common sense and ingenuity to the table.

The Commission believes priorities need to be set in education funding: all current expenditures should be reallocated to support the academic activities of the school. Education dollars should be spent on academics first and foremost. Budgets should distinguish between education and non-education activities.

At the same time, extending the envelope of the school day and year opens up the possibility of using funds in different ways. Federal compensatory funds, as we have suggested, can be employed to extend the school day and provide summer opportunities for those who require more time. Extended-day and other community services can be supported by other units of state and local government. Moreover, the costs of extended services can be partially met by modest fees, based on parental ability to pay. And costs can be controlled by carefully phasing in new services, using student-teachers and noncertified personnel, and making greater use of full-time staff on flexible schedules.

It should be noted that across the United States the ratio of adults to enrolled students exceeds one to ten, according to data from the National Center for Education Statistics.[3] Surely it is possible to restructure adult use of time so that more teachers and administrators actually encounter students on a daily basis in the classroom, face to face. This does not require additional money.

Throughout this document, the Commission has asked the question: Is there a better way? As these models demonstrate, visionary school leaders in districts of all kinds—large and small, wealthy and poor, urban and rural—are already supporting many of the reforms we advocate. These districts are financing the kinds of changes needed today to anticipate the challenges the future will place before us.

Several things are clear from these models. Many different alternative calendars do exist, most attuned to local needs. Parental choice is a significant feature of most of these models. Fees for additional services are charged in many of these alternatives. Above all, communities of all kinds face a powerful, pent-up demand for new and different educational services.

In the final analysis, the true costs depend on what we think is important. If we value learning, the cost of "doing it right the first time" is less than the expense involved in "doing it wrong" and having to do it over again. As the American business community now understands full well, in the end quality costs less.

---

3 "Adults" includes district staff, school administrators, teachers, instructional aides, guidance counselors, librarians and support staff.

FACING THE TEST OF TIME

Eleven years ago, a small booklet, *A Nation at Risk*, launched one of the great reform movements in American public life. It changed the terms of the education debate by urging education leaders to look beyond the details of schooling to three big issues: time, content, and expectations.

The response was dramatic and sustained. Expectations for student performance have been raised markedly—the public expects more, and so, too, do teachers and principals. Content standards are in the midst of drastic revision that holds out the promise of a world-class education for all.

But learning remains a prisoner of time. The description of the problem contained in *A Nation at Risk* is still true: "Compared to other nations, American students spend less time on school work; and time spent in the classroom and on homework is often used ineffectively." For practical people, reforming expectations and content were thought to be easier problems to solve; time, a more difficult issue to tackle. But in terms of learning, time as an elastic resource is the main road to excellence.

Americans can justifiably take pride in all they have accomplished and are trying to accomplish through their schools. We have built a remarkable system of public education through twelfth grade, universally available to all. We have provided access to postsecondary education at levels matched by no other nation. We have led the world in attending to the needs of the disadvantaged, the dispossessed, and the disabled. We are in the midst of the longest, sustained education reform movement since the common school was created in the 19th century.

Today a new challenge beckons: we must face the test of time. "Time," said Aeschylus 25 centuries ago, "teaches all things." Now at last we must learn its lesson about education: American students will have their best chance at success when they are no longer serving time, but when time is serving them.

APPENDICES

A.   MEMBERS OF COMMISSION

B.   ACKNOWLEDGMENTS

C.   SCHEDULE OF COMMISSION EVENTS

D.   WITNESSES: MEETINGS AND HEARINGS

E.   SITE VISITS

F   FOREIGN ITINERARIES

G.   GLOSSARY

MEMBERS OF THE NATIONAL EDUCATION COMMISSION ON TIME AND LEARNING

John Hodge Jones,
Murfreesboro, Tennessee

Jones is Commission chairman and school superintendent in Murfreesboro, Tennessee. Under his leadership, the school system has implemented a nationally recognized extended-day and -year program.

Carol Schwartz,
Washington, D. C.

Vice chairman of the Commission, Schwartz has served on the District of Columbia Board of Education and City Council. She has been a special education teacher and a consultant to the U.S. Department of Education.

Michael J. Barrett,
Cambridge, Massachusetts

Barrett represents four communities in the Massachusetts Senate. His 1990 cover story in *The Atlantic* helped spark a national debate about extending the school year.

B. Marie Byers,
Hagerstown, Maryland

A former teacher, Mrs. Byers is serving her 24th year on the Washington County Board of Education and is chair of the National School Board Association's Large District Forum. In 1990-91 she was president of the Maryland Association of Boards of Education.

Christopher T. Cross,
Washington, D.C.

Cross is director of the Education Initiative of The Business Roundtable and a member of the Maryland State Board of Education. He is a former assistant secretary for educational research and improvement in the U.S. Department of Education.

Denis P. Doyle,
Chevy Chase, Maryland

Doyle is a senior fellow at the Hudson Institute and was formerly with the American Enterprise Institute. A political scientist, he writes extensively about education policy and school reform.

Norman E. Higgins,
Guilford, Maine

A former teacher, Higgins is principal of Piscataquis Community High School. He has served on Maine's Common Core of Learning Commission and, in 1988, earned a National Alliance for the Arts Leadership Award.

William E. Shelton,
Ypsilanti, Michigan

A former teacher and principal, Shelton is president of Eastern Michigan University. He is active in local and national organizations and has written on higher education issues.

Glenn R. Walker,
Clyde, Kansas

Walker is a former teacher and Fulbright fellow. He is principal of Clifton-Clyde High School and Clifton Elementary School. From 1987 to 1991 Walker was state chairman of the "Initiative for Understanding: US-USSR Youth Exchange."

APPENDIX B

ACKNOWLEDGMENTS

The Commission wants to express its gratitude for the contributions of many individuals and organizations whose assistance made this report possible.

Our first acknowledgment goes to the elected officials who conceived of the need for this investigation, particularly the major legislative sponsor Senator Jeff Bingaman (New Mexico), and co-sponsors Senators Edward M. Kennedy (Massachusetts), Claiborne Pell (Rhode Island), Paul Simon (Illinois) and Mark O. Hatfield (Oregon), and Representatives William D. Ford and Dale E. Kildee of Michigan. They were ahead of their time in understanding that time is the missing piece in the education reform puzzle.

We also want to thank Secretary of Education Richard W. Riley for his interest in our work and his continuing support in the form of funding, and providing critical staff assistance from the Department of Education. In addition, we note the unflagging backing of the Commission's work by former Secretary of Education Lamar Alexander, Senators Robert Dole (Kansas), John Glenn (Ohio), George J. Mitchell (Maine), Paul S. Sarbanes (Maryland), and Representatives Barney Frank (Massachusetts), William F. Goodling (Pennsylvania), James M. Jeffords (Vermont), Joseph P. Kennedy II (Massachusetts), and the late William H. Natcher (Kentucky).

The vision of these public officials inspired us throughout our work.

We cannot adequately acknowledge the contributions of the 150 people who took the time to testify at the Commission's various meetings in the United States or to meet with us in Germany and Japan. They came from all walks of life—students, parents, teachers, administrators, researchers, analysts, and government officials. Their appeals were powerful and their insights compelling. If we have not done justice to their convictions, the faults is ours, because all expressed their views forcefully and well.

Many other people responded to our surveys and volunteered information about our charge. We are in their debt. Debra Hollinger served as our Designated Federal Official. Dena Stoner of the Council for Educational Development and Research provided continuing support.

We particularly appreciate the contributions of the capable and hard-working staff that helped guide our work. Commission Director Milton Goldberg's experience as former executive director of the National Commission on Excellence in Education and director of the National Institute of Education continually shaped our thinking. We could not have functioned without Deputy Executive Director Julia Anna Anderson. She kept us focused on our objectives and her understanding of the mysteries of the U.S. Department of Education was critical to the Commission's work.

Cheryl Kane, who directed our research effort, performed a prodigious feat in synthesizing knowledge about the complex topic of time and learning. With the help of other Commission staff, Dr. Kane was tireless in preparing materials, responding to our many demands, and checking our interpretations. Nelson Ashline provided valuable insights on the state role in education. Paul Gagnon made major contributions to our understanding of the standards movement and American curriculum compared to curriculum overseas. Joseph Teresa analyzed hearing testimony and prepared syntheses of the hearings. Anita Madan Renton compiled materials on international comparisons and innovative school programs. Frederick Edelstein provided early assistance with external relations.

Our support staff never failed us. Emma Madison Jordan (administrative officer), Patricia Roberson (receptionist and secretary) and Rachel Rosner (student intern) tirelessly made sure we got from place to place, on time and with the right agenda. Carol Copple, Douglas Levin, and David Nohara of Pelavin Associates, Washington, D.C., provided valuable research and analysis throughout the Commission's life.

Finally, we want to acknowledge the help of James Harvey who worked with Commission members Denis Doyle and Norman Higgins as principal draftsman of this report. Bruce Boston and Peter Slavin of James Harvey & Associates, Washington, D.C., helped with the report's development—Mr. Boston with drafting and Mr. Slavin with editing. The report was designed by Ellen F. Burns and Ken Cosgrove of Carter/Cosgrove, Alexandria, Virginia.

APPENDIX C

EVENT	DATE(S)	PLACE	HOST
Full Commission Meeting	April 13, 1992	Washington, DC	
Full Commission Meeting	May 15, 1992	Washington, DC	
Full Commission Meeting	June 25, 1992	Washington, DC	
Hearing	June 26, 1992	Washington, DC	
Full Commission Meeting	September 24, 1992	Washington, DC	
Hearing & Site Visits	October 22-23, 1992	Murfreesboro, TN	Murfreesboro City Schools
Full Commission Meeting	December 10, 1992	Washington, DC	
Hearing & Site Visits	January 14-15, 1993	Albuquerque, NM	Albuquerque Public Schools
Hearing & Site Visits	March 24, 1993	Oakland, CA	Beacon Day & Beacon High School
Hearing & Site Visit	March 25-26, 1993	Santa Monica, CA	Santa Monica Public Schools
Hearing & Site Visit	April 29-30, 1993	Ypsilanti, MI	Eastern Michigan University
Full Commission Meeting	May 13, 1993	Washington, DC	
Hearing & Site Visit	June 17-18, 1993	Lawrence, KS	University of Kansas
Hearing & Site Visit	September 22, 1993	Orono, ME	University of Maine
Hearing	September 23-24, 1993	Cambridge, MA	Harvard Graduate School of Education
Hearing and Site Visits	October 29, 1993	Annandale, VA	Fairfax County Public Schools
Fact-Finding Foreign Visits	December 3-10, 1993	Germany and Japan	Ministers of Education
Hearing and Site Visits	January 6-7, 1994	Hagerstown, MD	Washington County School District
Full Commission Meeting	February 4, 1994	Washington, DC	
Full Commission Meeting	February 28, 1994	Washington, DC	
Full Commission Meeting	March 4, 1994	Washington, DC	

APPENDIX D

WITNESSES: MEETINGS AND HEARINGS

JUNE 26, 1992
WASHINGTON, DC

Gordon Ambach, Executive Director, Council of Chief State School Officers, Washington, DC

Ralph Archibald, Superintendent of Schools, Marion County, FL (President, National Association for Year-Round Education)

Lillian Brinkley, President, National Association of Elementary School Principals, Alexandria, VA

James Dyke, Secretary of Education, Commonwealth of Virginia, Richmond, VA

Jeanne Griffith, Associate Commissioner, National Center for Education Statistics, Washington, DC

R. David Hall, President and Ward 2 Representative, District of Columbia School Board, Washington, DC

Nancy Mead, Director, International Assessment of Educational Progress, Educational Testing Service, Princeton, NJ

Harold Stevenson, Professor of Developmental Psychology, University of Michigan, Ann Arbor, MI

Bruce Walborn, International Association of Amusement Parks and Attractions, Alexandria, VA

SEPTEMBER 24, 1992
WASHINGTON, DC

Joyce Epstein, Co-Director, Center on Families, Communities, Schools, and Children's Learning, The Johns Hopkins University, Baltimore, MD

Robert Spillane, Superintendent, Fairfax County Public Schools, Fairfax, VA

Gene Wilhoit, Executive Director, National Association of State Boards of Education, Alexandria, VA

OCTOBER 22-23, 1992
MURFREESBORO, TENNESSEE

Beth Atkins, Extension Agent, Urban 4-H, University of Tennessee Agricultural Extension Service, Nashville, TN

Jerry Benefield, President and CEO, Nissan Motor Manufacturing Corp., USA, Murfreesboro, TN

Becci Bookner, Director, Extended School Program and Community Education, Murfreesboro Public Schools, Murfreesboro, TN

Sue Bordine, Assistant Principal, Mitchell-Neilson Elementary School, Murfreesboro, TN

Bev Callaway, League of Women Voters, Murfreesboro, TN

Joel Jobe, Managing Partner, Jobe, Turley, and Associates, Murfreesboro, TN

Monica Lewis, Director, Extended School, Bedford County Board of Education, Bedford County, TN

Wendy Day Rowell, ESP Parent, Mitchell-Neilson Elementary School, Murfreesboro, TN

Ralph Vaughn, Executive Director, Rutherford/Murfreesboro Chamber of Commerce, Murfreesboro, TN

Jane Williams, Director, Professional Laboratory Experiences, Middle Tennessee State University, Murfreesboro, TN

Richard Benjamin, Director of Schools, Metropolitan-Nashville Public Schools, Nashville, TN

David Brittain, Chief, Bureau of Education Technology, Florida Department of Education, Tallahassee, FL

Carolyn Evertson, Chair, Department of Teaching and Learning, Vanderbilt University, Nashville, TN

Russell L. French, Bureau of Educational Research and Service, University of Tennessee, Knoxville, TN

Willis Hawley, Center for Educational Policy, Vanderbilt Institute of Public Policy Studies, Nashville, TN

Gary Middleton, Deputy Regional Vice President, State Farm Insurance Company, South Central Region, Murfreesboro, TN

William Page, President, Insignia Financial Group, Inc., Greenville, SC

Gail Walker, Kindergarten Teacher, Konnoak Elementary School, Winston-Salem, NC

Elaine Willers, Director, Tennessee Academy for School Leaders, Tennessee State Department of Education, Nashville, TN

DECEMBER 10, 1992
WASHINGTON, DC

Sarah Huyvaert, Professor, Eastern Michigan University, Ypsilanti, MI

JANUARY 14-15, 1993
ALBUQUERQUE, NEW MEXICO

Tom Burnett, Director, Christopher Columbus Consortium, Apple Computers, Austin, TX

Cindy Chapman, Teacher, Longfellow Elementary
School, Albuquerque, NM

Donald Davidson, Vice President, Jostens Learning
Corporation, San Diego, CA

Geraldine Harge, Assistant Superintendent,
Albuquerque Public Schools, Albuquerque, NM

Kurt Steinhaus, Director of Education Planning and
Technology, State Department of Education,
Santa Fe, NM

Virginia Trujillo, President, New Mexico State Board
of Education, Albuquerque, NM

Pauline Turner, Assistant Dean of Education,
University of New Mexico, Albuquerque, NM

Sandra Graham, Graduate School of Education,
University of California at Los Angeles,
Los Angeles, CA

James Greeno, School of Education. Stanford
University, Palo Alto, CA

Amado Padilla, School of Education, Stanford
University, Palo Alto, CA

Susanna Purnell, RAND Corporation,
Santa Monica, CA

JANUARY 28-29, 1993
WASHINGTON, DC

Malcolm Skilbeck, Deputy Director for Education,
Directorate for Education, Employment, Labor and
Social Affairs, Organization for Economic
Cooperation and Development, Paris, France

MARCH 24, 1993
OAKLAND, CALIFORNIA

Lisa Hotaling, Student, Beacon High School

Nathan Inwood, Student, Beacon High School

Josh Roth, Student, Beacon High School

Rima Ransom, Student, Beacon High School

Scott Rostoni, Student, Sir Francis Drake High
School, San Anselmo, CA

Michelle Swanson, Teacher, Sir Francis Drake High
School, San Anselmo, CA

Kiel Harkness, Student, Beacon High School

Samara Dictor, Student, Beacon High School

Galen Moore, Student, Beacon High School

Zuiho Taniguchi, Student, Beacon High School

Daisuke Muro, Student, Beacon High School

Adrian Bozzolo, Parent, Beacon High School

Oliana Sadler, Parent, Beacon High School

Nancy Springer, Teacher, Beacon High School

Julie Fuller, Beacon Day School Student

Jordan Reynolds, Beacon Day School Student

Hannah Roth, Beacon Day School Student

Kate Newlin, Beacon Day School Student

Noah Finneburgh, Beacon Day School Student

Colin Gage, Beacon Day School Student

Judy Yeager, Parent, Beacon Day School

Edd Conboy, Parent, Beacon Day School

Julee Richardson, Parent, Beacon Day School

Lana Harkness, Beacon Day School Teacher

MARCH 25-26, 1993
SANTA MONICA, CALIFORNIA

Neil Schmidt, Superintendent, Santa Monica Unified
Public Schools, Santa Monica, CA

Norman Brekke, Superintendent, Oxnard Public
School District, Oxnard, CA

Jane Zykowski, Year-Round Education Project,
University of California at Riverside, Riverside, CA

Leslie Medine, Co-Director, Beacon Day & High
School, Oakland, CA

Michelle Swanson, Teacher, Sir Francis Drake High
School, San Anselmo, CA

Sharon Conley, Professor, College of Education,
University of Arizona, Tucson, AZ

Stephen Heyneman, Chief, Human Resources
Division, The World Bank, Washington, DC

Jacquelyn McCroskey, Professor, School of Social
Work, University of Southern California,
Los Angeles, CA

Lawrence Picus, Associate Director, Center for
Research in Education Finance, University of
Southern California, Los Angeles, CA

APRIL 29-30, 1993
YPSILANTI, MICHIGAN

Valerie Mills, Public School Teacher, Ypsilanti, MI

Carol Polkinghorn, National Education Association
Time Commission, Greensburg Salem, PA

Beverly Campbell, Public School Teacher, Detroit, MI

Nathaniel Reid, Program Coordinator, Center for Occupational & Personalized Education, Ann Arbor, MI

James Kelly, Chief Executive Officer, National Boards for Professional Teaching Standards, Detroit, MI

Judith Lanier, President, Michigan Partnership for New Education, East Lansing, MI

Dennis Sparks, Executive Director, National Staff Development Council, Dearborn, MI

Jerry Robbins, Dean, College of Education, Eastern Michigan University, Ypsilanti, MI

MAY 13, 1993
WASHINGTON, DC

Anthony de Souza, National Geographic Society, Washington, DC

David Florio, National Academy of Sciences, National Research Council, Washington, DC

Harold Pratt, National Academy of Sciences, National Research Council, Washington, DC

James Gates, National Council of Teachers of Mathematics, Reston, VA

Paul Lehman, Music Educators National Conference, Reston, VA

Miles Myers, National Council of Teachers of English, Champaign, IL

JUNE 17-18, 1993
LAWRENCE, KANSAS

Charles Greenwood, Director, Juniper Gardens Children's Project, University of Kansas, Lawrence, KS

Marlin Berry, Superintendent, Smoky Valley Public Schools, Lindsborg, KS

Marvin Kaiser, Associate Dean, College of Arts and Sciences, Kansas State University, Manhattan, KS

Robert Wehling, Vice President for Public Affairs, Proctor & Gamble, Cincinnati, OH

Honorable Sam Brownback, Secretary of Agriculture, Kansas State Board of Agriculture, Topeka, KS

Brice B. Durbin, Former Executive Director, National Federation of State High School Associations, Topeka, KS

Marcia McFarland, Extension Specialist, 4-H and Youth Program, Kansas State University, Manhattan, KS

SEPTEMBER 22, 1993
ORONO, MAINE

Polly Ward, Maine Deputy Commissioner of Education, Augusta, ME

Donna Vigue, English Teacher and Curriculum Consultant for Project 2000, Piscataquis Community High School, Guilford, ME

Pamela Rolfe, English Teacher and member of Standards Project, Caribou, ME

Marjorie Medd, Chairman, State Board of Education, Norway, ME

SEPTEMBER 23-24, 1993
CAMBRIDGE, MASSACHUSETTS

Jerry Murphy, Dean, Harvard Graduate School of Education, Cambridge, MA

Harold Howe, Senior Lecturer Emeritus, Harvard Graduate School of Education, Cambridge, MA

Ted Sanders, Superintendent of Public Instruction, Ohio State Department of Education, Columbus, OH

Susan Fuhrmann, Co-Director, Consortium for Policy Research in Education, Eagleton Institute, Rutgers University, New Brunswick, NJ

Henry Levin, Director of Accelerated Schools Project, Stanford University, Palo Alto, CA

Robert Slavin, Director of Elementary School Programs, John Hopkins University, Baltimore, MD

Patricia Albjerg Graham, President, Spenser Foundation, Chicago, IL

Theodore Sizer, Chairman of the Coalition of Essential Schools, Brown University, Providence, RI

Richard Elmore, Professor of Education, Harvard Graduate School of Education, Cambridge, MA

Edward Zigler, Sterling Professor of Psychology, Yale University, New Haven, CT

OCTOBER 29, 1993
ANNANDALE, VIRGINIA

Robert R. Spillane, Superintendent, Fairfax County Public Schools, Fairfax, VA

William R. Thomas, Coordinator Technology Services, Chapel Square Center, Annandale, VA

Marianne O'Brien, Technology Coordinator 9-12, Chapel Square Center, Annandale, VA

Fran Gallagher, Technology Coordinator K-8, Chapel Square Center, Annandale, VA

Bill Reeder, Coordinator, Integrated Technology Services, Chapel Square Center, Annandale, VA

Linda Sue Dauphin, Coordinator, Library Automation and Information Services, Chapel Square Center, Annandale, VA

Pam Miles, Teacher Services Specialist, Chapel Square Center, Annandale, VA

Terry Woolsey, Electronic Classroom and Educational Television Specialist, Chapel Square Center, Annandale, VA

ALEXANDRIA, VIRGINIA

Geoffrey Jones, Principal, Thomas Jefferson High School for Science and Technology

Claire Voskuhl, Parent, Thomas Jefferson High School for Science and Technology

Seth Mitcho, Student, Thomas Jefferson High School for Science and Technology

Lauren Hale, Student, Thomas Jefferson High School for Science and Technology

Nicole Neuschler, Student, Thomas Jefferson High School for Science and Technology

Erin Neuschler, Student, Thomas Jefferson High School for Science and Technology

Paul Helms, Student, Thomas Jefferson High School for Science and Technology

JANUARY 6-7, 1994
HAGERSTOWN, MARYLAND

David Hornbeck, Education Consultant, Baltimore, MD

Margaret Trader, Associate Superintendent, Washington County Public Schools, Hagerstown, MD

Michael Riley, Associate Superintendent, Baltimore County Schools, Baltimore, MD

Jay McTighe, Education Consultant, Frederick County, MD

Paul Brunelle, Executive Director, Maine Association of Boards of Education, Augusta, ME

Carolyn Seburn, Supervisor of Research & Testing, Washington County Public Schools, Hagerstown, MD

John Davidson, Supervisor of Computer Instruction and Technology, Hagerstown, MD

APPENDIX E

SITE VISITS

Beacon Day and High School
2101 Livingston Street
Oakland, CA 94606
Leslie Medine, Co-Director

Carl Sandburg Intermediate School
8428 Fort Hunt Road
Alexandria, VA 22308
Linda Whitfield, Principal

Carl Taylor Elementary School
2120 Taylor Avenue
North Odgen, UT 85501
Reed Spencer, Principal

Chapel Square Technology Center
4414 Holborn St.
Annandale, VA 22003
William Thomas, Coordinator

Emerson Elementary School
620 Georgia SE
Albuquerque, NM 87108
Anna Marie Ulibarri, Principal

Eastern Elementary School
1320 Yale Drive
Hagerstown, MD 21742
Patricia Dell, Principal

Governor Bent Elementary School
5700 Hendrix Road, NE
Albuquerque, NM 87110
Marilyn Davenport, Principal

Hefferan Elementary School
4409 West Wilcox
Chicago, IL 60624
Patricia Harvey, Principal

International Children's Home
500 S. Lamborn
Helena, MT 59601
Claudia Morley, Director

James A. Foshay Middle School
3751 South Harvard Boulevard
Los Angeles, CA 90018
Howard Lappin, Principal

Leadville School District
107 Spruce Street - P. O. Box 977
Leadville, CO 80461
Jim McCabe, Superintendent

Mooresville School District
305 N. Main Street - P. O. Box 119
Mooresville, NC 28115
Jane Carrigan, Superintendent

Murfreesboro Extended School Program
400 N. Maple Street, P.O. Box 279
Murfreesboro, TN 37133-0279
Becci Bookner, Director

New Stanley Elementary School
36th & Metropolitan
Kansas City, KS 66106
Donna Hardy, Principal

Park View Optional Year-Round School
251 West McNeely Avenue
Mooresville, NC 28115
Roger Hyatt, Principal

Parry McCluer High School
2329 Chestnut Avenue
Buena Vista, VA 24416
Wayne Flint, Principal

Piscataquis Community High School
P. O. Box 118 (Blane Avenue)
Guilford, ME 04443
Norman Higgins, Principal

Salt Lake City Community High School
180 North 300 West
Salt Lake City, UT 84103
James Anderson, Principal

Sir Francis Drake High School
1327 Sir Francis Drake Blvd.
San Anselmo, CA 94960
Michelle Swanson, Program Coordinator

The Cornerstone Schools Association
305 Michigan Avenue
Detroit, MI 48226
Norma Henry, Principal

Thomas Jefferson High School
6560 Braddock Road
Alexandria, VA 22312
Geoffrey Jones, Principal

Washington County School District
Commonwealth Avenue (P.O. Box 730)
Hagerstown, MD 21740
Wayne Gersen, Superintendent

FOREIGN ITINERARIES

GERMANY

Government Officials

Karsten Brenner, Director, Federal Ministry of Education and Science, Bonn

Werner Nagel, Secretariat of the Standing Conference of the Ministers of Education and Cultural Affairs of the Länder in the FRG, Bonn

Norbert Lammert, Parliamentary State Secretary, Bonn

Gisela Morel-Tiernann, Secretariat of the Standing Conference of the Ministers of Education and Cultural Affairs of the Länder in the Federal Republic of Germany, Bonn

Hans-Jürgen Pokall, Berlin Senate Administration for Schools, Vocational Training and Sports, Berlin

Hartmut Holzapfel, Minister of Education of the State of Hesse

Hermann Schmidt, Federal Institute of Vocational Training, Berlin

Ulrike Grassau, Senate Administration for Schools, Vocational Training and Sports, Berlin

Brigitte Zaschke, Federal Ministry of Education and Science, Bonn

Researchers

Wolfgang Mitter, Director, German Institute for International Educational Research, Frankfurt

Peter Dobrich, German Institute for International Educational Resarch, Frankfurt

Peter M. Roeder, Max Planck Institute for Human Development and Education, Berlin

Manfred Weiss, German Institute for International Education Research, Frankfurt

Ines Graudenz, German Institute for International Education Research, Frankfurt

Dirk Randoll, German Institute for International Education Research, Frankfurt

Clive IIopes, German Institute for International Education Research, Frankfurt

Wolfgang IIuck, German Institute for International Education Research, Frankfurt

School Principals

Mr. Doms, Director, Vocational School for Telecommunications, Berlin

Charles C. Hanna, Managing Principal, John Kennedy School, Berlin

George Hoffmann, Director, Vocational School for Precision Engineering, Berlin

Volker Dingelday, Head of Bettinaschule (Gymnasium), Frankfurt am Main

Heidi Bachmeyer, Head of Münzenberger-Schule (Primary School), Frankfurt am Main

Armin Lohmann, Head of Steinwaldschule (Integrated Comprehensive), Nuekirchen

Bodo Uhlmann, Head of Grund-Haupt-und Realschule, Frielendorf-Verna

Embassy of the United States of America

Robert Allen Sarofeen, First Secretary-Administration, United States Embassy, Berlin

Brigitta Birke-Dexheimer, Educational Advisor, United States Embassy (USIS), Bonn

Katherine L. Wood, Second Secretary, United States Embassy, Berlin

Angela Buhring, Cultural Affairs Assistant, United States Embassy (USIS), Bonn

JAPAN

Ministry of Education, Science and Culture (Monbusho)

Tetsuo Tsujimura, Deputy Director-General, Elementary and Secondary Education Bureau

Takashi Yamagiwa, Chief School Inspector, Elementary and Secondary Education Bureau

Hiroki Yoshitake, Planning Director, Curriculum, Elementary and Secondary Education Bureau

Masakatsu Oikawa, Deputy Director, Teacher Training Division, Local Education Support Bureau

Shigeki Wakabayashi, Senior Specialist, Development Cooperation, Education and Cultural Exchange Office, Science and International Affairs Bureau

Robert Juppe, JET Advisor, The Upper Secondary School Division, Elementary and Secondary Education Bureau

Takako Yoshino, Programme Officer, Educational and Cultural Exchange Office

National Institute for Education Research

Reiki Kijima, Director, Department of General Affairs

Professor Masami Maki, Director, Research Department of Educational Management

Professor Seiji Inoue, Head, Office of Overall Planning and Coordination

Professor Eizo Nagasaki, Head, Research Division of Mathematics Education

Takanori Sakamoto, Senior Researcher, Department of Overall Planning and Coordination

Professor Atsushi Katoh, Researcher, Research Division of Guidance and Counseling

Saitama Prefectural Board of Education

Mr. Ozaki, Deputy Director, Educational Policy Office

Shin Shinotsuka, Director, Guidance Department

Koichi Kawata, Senior Teacher Consultant

Tokyo and Japan Chamber of Commerce

Takasi Sakuragi, General Manager, Planning and Researching Division

Hideaki Tanaka, Planning and Researching Division Project Manager

Mariko Mori, Planning and Researching Division

Hidekazu Ohshita, Planning and Researching Division

Hirosi Ohuchi, Planning and Researching Division

National Olympic Memorial Youth Center

Shigeo Ohno, President, The Harmony Center (Organization for Child Development) C/O National Olympic Memorial Youth Center

Hiroo Sueyoshi, Executive Director, National Federation of Kodomo-kai

KAWAIJUKU

Hiroto Kawai, Vice Chairman, KAWAIJUKU, Kawaijuku Educational Institution, Nagoya, Japan

Kaishinn-Daisan Elementary School

Takeo Kikuchi, Principal

Tetsuji Koseki, Teacher

Kazuyuki Terashima, Teacher

Hiroto Shimazaki, Teacher

Chikashi Ooe, Teacher Consultant, Nerima Ward Board of Education

Miyoji Kobayashi, Supervisor of Nerima Board of Education

Madea Butts, Student

Tomoko Uwatoko, Student

Tokyo Metropolitan Hakuo Senior High School

Shouji Kayahara, Principal

Fukushima Prefectural Board of Education

Senichi Watanabe, Deputy Superintendent of Education

Koichiro Minato, Section Chief, General Affairs Division

Kazushige Yamashita, Division Chief, General Affairs Division

Tetsuya Watabe, Senior Staff, General Affairs Division

Nosan Senior High School

Torahachiro Ohtake, Principal

Joho Junior High School

Akio Konno, Principal

Interpreter

Noriko Iwamoto, Toshima-ku, Tokyo

Embassy of the United States of America

Paul P. Blackburn, Minister-Counselor of Embassy for Public Affairs

Charles Walsh, First Secretary for Cultural Affairs

Mikiko Matsumoto, Cultural Affairs Assistant.

Abitur: A rigorous academic examination German students must pass prior to acceptance at a university.

Academic Day: That part of the day the Commission believes should be reserved for study in the core academic curriculum.

Core Academic Curriculum: The Commission defines the following as the core academic curriculum that all students should take during the academic day: English and language arts, mathematics, science, civics, geography, history, the arts, and foreign languages.

Design Flaw: Permitting standards to vary among students while keeping time constant instead of providing each student the time needed to reach high standards.

Juku: Private Japanese tutorial schools that supplement school learning, offer remedial and enrichment experiences, and prepare students for university examinations.

National Education Goals: Goals first adopted by the nation's governors in 1989 for attainment by the year 2000. The goals have been incorporated into GOALS 2000: Educate America Act. (See "Dimensions of the Time Challenge" for description of the goals.)

Out-of-School Learning: Skills, knowledge, habits and perspectives students acquire outside the walls of the school through participation in family and community environments.

School Day: The total time students are in school, including the academic day (see above) and the time before or after the academic day during which students engage in subjects outside the core academic curriculum, receive supplementary educational services, and participate in extracurricular activities.

World-Class Standards: Standards for student learning and performance that will permit American students to match or exceed the performance of students in other countries.

Year-Round Schools: An alternative to the traditional nine-month school calendar. The 180-day school year is broken into instructional blocks that are staggered throughout the year. The days customarily devoted to the typical summer vacation are divided into several "mini-vacations" called Intersessions that are spread out over the calendar year. For example, a student might be in school for twelve weeks, on vacation during a four-week Intersession, and back in school for another twelve-week period. Additional instructional time may or may not be provided during the intersessions for the purposes of enrichment or remedial work.

Single-Track Year-Round Schools: A plan in which all students attend school on the same schedule of instructional sessions and vacations.

Multi-Track Year-Round Schools. A plan in which students in one school are divided into three, four, or five groups, each with different schedules of instructional and vacation time. The time students spend in schools is staggered so that one group is on vacation while other groups are in school. Multi-track schools have been created primarily to deal with overcrowding and to make better use of facilities.